T0065156

God

Old Questions
New Answers

F.B. Enn

Order this book online at www.trafford.com
or email orders@trafford.com

Most Trafford titles are also available at major online book retailers.

Print information available on the last page.

ISBN: 978-1-6987-1435-6 (sc)
ISBN: 978-1-6987-1437-0 (hc)
ISBN: 978-1-6987-1436-3 (e)

Library of Congress Control Number: 2023906501

Trafford rev. 04/06/2023

www.trafford.com
North America & international
toll-free: 844-688-6899 (USA & Canada)
fax: 812 355 4082

Preface

This book is about the author's perspectives regarding God, based on logic, science, and religion.

This book is formatted in question-and-answer style such that readers can jump quickly to author's answers for those questions regarding God which readers may considered still unanswered or known answers not making sense.

Why believe in God? If God exist, how does God govern this universe, why God took that long to create this universe and us, why all those suffering despite those believe and obedience? Why do we have to obey God if we know what's good or bad for ourselves? Is our fate already determined by God? Why and how God destined our death? Why punish non-believer in Hell if God is forgiving, merciful and loving? How do we know God is not man-made? These are examples of questions from the 28 questions posed in this book.

This book will provide readers with answers which might be different, not commonly told previously to invite readers to a fresh, new level of understanding God, as supported by logic, science, and religious texts. These are new answers to old questions regarding God.

This book may also be perceived to contain controversial texts, but please keep an open mind to continue and complete the reading such as not to be out of context.

Thank you and enjoy the reading.

F.B. Enn
April 2023

Contents

Q0: Before we discuss about God, can you tell us about yourself?

A: I am what I am.

I believe in seeking for the right way with logic, science, and religion but I don't claim myself to be a philosopher, scientist nor religious scholar.

I believe in seeking for the right way with open mind to be closer to the truth.

I believe the right way is "not gambling", not necessarily the absolute truth but there are net benefits even if I am wrong, not necessarily perfect (*as there will be no progress, no improvement with perception of perfection*) and the right way will remain right until proven wrong.

I believe the right way is to believe in God. I am here not to preach about religion or to convert people to a religion. I am here to defense God.

I am not a perfect Muslim; I am not representing Islam as my answer might be different. I am continually learning.

Q1: What do you mean by "not gambling"?

A: Not gambling, to me is choosing a way when I know it is <u>more likely</u> (*if not certainly*) to be true that there are net benefits in choosing that way even if I am wrong.

There are net benefits such that:

- If I am right, the benefits will outweigh the burdens and,
- If I am wrong, the benefits of the opportunities seized from the burdens will outweigh,
  - o any losses (*with or without the mitigation, including opportunity loss*) and,
  - o any burdens (*including burden of any mitigation work or proactive change of way before time of no return*).

Examples of the benefits of the opportunities that can be seized from the burdens that outweigh any losses (*excluding safety and health*) and burdens are firstly, safety and health benefits. What are those losses, burdens, or even other benefits if we are not safe and healthy (*including mental health*)? Secondly, records for learning to do better such that tomorrow's win is more than today's loss.

On the contrary, gambling is choosing a way when I know it is <u>less likely</u> (*if not impossible*) to be true that there are net benefits in choosing that way if I am either right or wrong.

Time of no return means the time when the decided way can no longer be changed.

"Don't know" means anything is possible or the probability to be true or false is 50/50. If I know something, but not certainly to be true, either known as more likely or less likely to be true, that is I "know", not I "don't know".

If I choose a way but I "don't know" the truth of that chosen way and any other probable ways and the chosen way is not changeable before time of no return, that is gambling.

If I choose a way that I "don't know" the truth of that chosen way, but I know that all other probable ways are less likely/impossible to be true, then it is also not gambling as my chosen way is now more likely to be true.

If I don't choose any way as I "don't know" the truth of any probable ways, that is undecisive. If I am undecisive till time of no return, that is gambling.

Gambling is to be deliberately avoided (*eschewed*) as per God's revelation in Appendix A:1.

Q2: How do you describe God?

A: Nothing like God.

God is a being with such will, knowledge, wisdom and power that created and govern this universe and lives with God's creation rules such as rule of pairs & continual testing and shape human being to be such distinct from other lives to serve God for the greater good.

God is so loving, merciful, forgiving, hearing, seeing and not injustice.

This description is derived and inferred from God's revelation as per Appendix A:2 – 18, A:44.

Others may describe God differently, but the common understanding is that God is so intelligent and powerful such that God created and govern this universe.

Q3: What is your evidence for existence of God?

A: There is no evidence of God if evidence constitute direct observation from our senses and/or experiment that conform with the description of God. However, there is also no evidence that there is no God as our senses and/or experiment, despite technologically aided, have yet to reach all parts inside this universe, let alone outside this universe, to observe God. Even if there is any of such observation, we will not know if what we observed is God or not God as Nothing like God as per God's revelation in Appendix A:2.

Q4: Why don't God just shows Himself up for people to believe?

A: Will those with so high intelligence and power really want to show themselves up to us?

Even those scientists who strongly believe in that intelligent and powerful alien have difficulty to provide hard evidence that there is such alien despite of the advanced telescope and scientific investigation such as by SETI (*Search Extraterrestrial Intelligence*) Institute and Ancient Aliens television series.

Why should God show Himself up to all, billions of people in this world, one by one, from the past, presence to the future? God could have just once-off programmed us to have that innate (*natural, inborn*) thinking that there is God after observing this universe, once-off revealed Himself through His revelation to us and let our freewill choose to believe Him or not to such extent, for the greater good.

Even if God show Himself up visibly, how do you know it's not that some people in this modern world will still not believe that is God as they will argue it's a hoax or that phenomena can be explained by science or it's an alien?

Even if we "wow" and believe God after seeing God (*assuming our eyes are permitted to see God safely*), how do you know it's not that some of us will stop their "wow" after continually seeing God as some human mind will never get enough?

We can know God with open heart and mind. God revealed that there are indeed signs for those who reflect as per God's revelation in Appendix A: 41.

Q5: If there is no evidence of God's existence or non-existence, how do you know that your belief in God is right?

A: It's like our grandfather. How do we know that our grandfather is our grandfather? Most likely, we don't do DNA test as evidence to know whether our grandfather is our grandfather, but we infer based on logic and the claim by our trusted father that our grandfather is our grandfather. So, our grandfather is more likely our grandfather, not absolutely our grandfather but we have somehow decided to believe him.

Truth can be known not only by evidence but also by logical inference. Although evidence can give absolute truth while logical inference can only give probability/likelihood of truth (*more likely* truth), for practical reason, in life, we normally, logically infer to believe it is true or false, especially when the evidence cannot be obtained timely or there is no benefit to get the evidence. Logical inference can be immediate and require no further time like evidence seeking to assess the truth.

We refer to our <u>knowledge of similar (*if not same*) event in other time and space</u> (KOSETS) to make logical inference. The probability of truth will depend on how the knowledge is acquired (*direct or indirect observation, from reliable or unreliable source*) and how similar is the event at that time and space to the claim made. With no absolute truth in logical inference, there is still a possibility that it may turn out to be not true.

For example, we logically infer that "Mr. A is <u>more likely</u> to have passed the examination as we have directly observed the official result (*the acquired knowledge*) that Mr. A had passed the mock/trial examination (*similar event*) last month (*in other time*)". With no absolute truth, there is still a possibility that Mr. A may has not passed the examination.

Logic can be common sense if the KOSETS is a common knowledge to the majority, if not all people. Logic can be logical to only certain people if only that certain people have the KOSETS.

Truth can also be, more likely, not absolutely, with the claim by trusted people (CTP). For example, when we visited a doctor to diagnose our sickness, we logically infer that it was more likely that the conclusion of the diagnosis was true as such conclusion by the doctor on our sickness is a CTP. But there were also times that the conclusion of such diagnosis was later found to be not true.

Sometimes, what we took for granted as evidence is actually the CTP and/or logical inference only. For example, the so-called evidence of Dark Matter. Did anyone directly observe the existence of Dark Matter? No. Scientist just logically infer the existence of Dark Matter from its presumed gravitational effect that help in the formation of galaxies. Could Dark Matter be actually not existing but instead due to our flawed understanding of gravity? Possible. Another example is the so-called evidence of Dark Energy. Did anyone directly observe the existence of Dark Energy? No. Scientist just logically infer the existence of Dark Energy from the expansion of the universe. Could Dark Energy be actually not existing but instead due to our flawed understanding of black holes? Possible. These are disputes among scientists now. Scientific knowledge is prone to be the CTP and/or logical inference only, but somehow, we tend to believe them, though the truth is not yet absolute.

With no absolute truth in either logical inference or CTP, we don't dismiss them straightaway, especially when the evidence cannot be obtained timely or there is no benefit to get the evidence. But instead, we generate all probable ways that are mutually exclusive and exhaustive. We consider the mitigative action should we are wrong and identify the opportunities in each way. We decide to accept/believe the way that is more likely (*if not certainly*) to be true that there are bigger net benefits compared to other probable ways i.e., the benefits outweigh the burdens if we are right, and the benefits of the opportunities seized also outweigh any losses and burdens if we are wrong. We later proactively change our decision if there are signs that we are wrong and that the mitigative actions won't work.

There are many logics and scientific theories/hypothesis that I can refer to logically infer that God is more likely to exist. And there are net benefits in believing in God. If I am wrong in my decision (*that God actually don't exist*), I just rest in peace after death and the benefits in safety and health with self-actualization of being giving, though with limited freedom/joy/pleasure, outweigh the burdens in believing in God and outweigh the opportunity losses of the unlimited freedom/joy/pleasure during my lifetime. But if I am right in my decision, I am set to Heaven.

On the other hand, if I am non-believer of God, I will rest in peace after death with unlimited freedom/joy/pleasure during my lifetime, if I am right. But if I am wrong, I will be eternally in Hell frying. So, there is no net benefit if I am wrong.

My believe in God is right until proven wrong.

Q6: Can you explain the logic and science that support your belief in God?

A: I am not gambling to believe in God as:

- The probability of God's existence is higher than the probability of God's non-existence,
- There are net benefits even if I am wrong to believe in God and,
- There is no hard evidence that God don't exist.

Let me first, tell the analogical story of the dice, then its connection to the logical, scientific observation of this universe, and later my conclusion on God's existence.

Mr. A saw text messages from an unknown person who called himself as God. He claimed that when he threw dice for 7 times, the number would be 1,1,1,1,1,1, X successively:

- For the purpose that Mr. A can easily recognize the <u>one</u> intelligent and powerful God,
- The letter X can vary from 1 to 6 based on present and past situation and,
- The ending of the throw after 7 times of throw is not in the hand of the dice, but in God's hand.

God said that if Mr. A believe and obey him, Mr. A will receive a gift. If not, Mr. A will receive a stick. So, Mr. A invited 7 other observers to observe the throwing with the thrower unseen. They had limited time to conclude their observation.

The dice was actually thrown out 7 times and the number actually turn out to be 1,1,1,1,1,1,1 successively.

The 1st observer said it's just luck. But the probability is (1/6 x 1/6 x 1/6 x 1/6 x 1/6 x 1/6 x 1/6) x 100% = (1/279,936) x 100% = 0.0003%, it's very small, so Mr. A believed it's very unlikely. Believing in such luck is gambling.

To make it more likely, mathematically, it requires 279,936 rounds of trial-and-error throws but what they saw was just one round of successful trial-and-error throws. Even the 279,936 rounds of throws will not certainly/guarantee make one of the rounds of throws to be successful, it's just more likely as it can be more or less than 279,936 rounds of trial-and-error throws to make one round of successful throw. The 1st observer argued that "We are just lucky, so appreciate it and move on". So, Mr. A asked, "Why are we lucky, and how else and then to be lucky? Who created or what caused such "lucky" throw?".

Then the 2nd observer said there were actually more or less, 279,936 rounds of trial-and-error throws happening simultaneously but it's all invisible except the one round that is visible which turned out to be the lucky one. So, Mr. A thought, "Is the 2nd observer dreaming?". However, to be open-minded, Mr. A believed this hypothesis could be true if there is evidence that the invisible throws were really happening. But Mr. A also thought it's less likely that Mr. A could get the evidence with limited time to conclude the observation. Even if it's true as Mr. A could get the evidence, then the question will be who created or what caused such invisible throws?

The 3rd observer said that their observations were just seeing movie and it can be proven. So, Mr. A thought, "Did the 3rd observer seeing too many video games?". However, to be open-minded, Mr. A believed this hypothesis could be true if there is evidence that there was a movie but Mr. A also thought it's less likely that Mr. A could get the evidence with limited time to conclude the observation. Even if it's true as Mr. A could get the evidence, then the question will be who created or what caused such movie?

The 4th observer said there were already more or less, 279,936 rounds of trial-and-error throws prior to the observation day of the lucky throw. The 4th observer said that, since the room was made available 4 years ago, there were more or less, 192 rounds of trial-and-error throws done per day since then. So, Mr. A thought, "Is the 4th observer realistic?". However, to be open-minded, Mr. A believed this hypothesis could be true if there was evidence that the trial-and-error throws were really happening but there was no continuous recording of the trial-and-error throws unless a time machine is made to go back to the past to continuously record the throws. So, Mr. A also thought it's less likely that Mr. A could get the evidence with limited time to conclude the observation. Even if it's true as Mr. A could get the evidence, then the question will be who created or what caused such trial-and-error throws?

The 5th observer said he could provide a scientific explanation by inventing the mathematic to discover the equation of natural forces acting on the dice that enable the number to be as such. He then came out with several mathematical equations and when the experimental observation could not exactly match his equation, he added more assumption and constant in his equation to match the observation. When asked, who created or what caused that equation of natural things, he said he will find the Theory of Everything to consolidate and simplify those equations. The Theory of Everything eventually came out and stated that each of the dices has all their faces having same number of 1 which can guarantee the intended result even if the natural things equations are wrong.

Then Mr. A asked who created or what caused such Theory of Everything, and the 5th observer said there must be a scientific explanation to be proven later but it could not be that God explanation. If so, the question is who created or what caused such dice design or scientific mechanism/equation/law?

The scientific explanation, except those with probabilistic variables, explained a definite pattern with accurate predictable outcome. However, currently, the scientific explanation, although tested to be true, provided only the immediate cause and mechanism/equation/ law, but not the root cause or source of the event.

The root cause or source of the event is hereby called the "Ultimate Creator" (UC). Currently, the UC is beyond the reach of science. Perhaps in the future, science can explain the UC but there is limited time to conclude the observation and logic must be relied upon here to address the question of the UC.

All the 1st, 2nd, 3rd, 4th, 5th observer's hypothesis/theory were either less likely to be true, less likely to be proven in the limited time to conclude the observation or even if it is true, the question is who created or what caused such "lucky" throw or invisible throws or movie or trial-and-error throws or dice design or scientific mechanism/equation/law? The answer here is ultimately the UC.

The UC is either one of the following mutually exclusive and exhaustive 4 possible entities of "Ultimate Creator" (4PEUC), i.e.:

- Nothing (UC),
- Something (UC),
- God (UC),
- An entity of any possible sequence of creation between Nothing, Something and God prior to the direct causation of the dice throwing such as:
  o Nothing (UC) created Something,
  o Nothing (UC) created God,
  o Something (UC) created God,
  o God (UC) created Something,
  o Something (UC) created God created Something,
  o Nothing (UC) created Something created God,
  o Nothing (UC) created God created Something.
  o Nothing (UC) created Something created God created Something.

Note:

1. *Something can be singular or multiple sequence of creation of variations of something, e.g., Something1 created Something2 created Something3, etc.*
2. *Entity is thing with independent and distinct existence.*

Mr. A then inferred that the true entity among the 4PEUC was more likely to be intelligent than rather non-intelligent. Why?

As by definition, intelligence can be characterized by the following, so the intelligent creator and its intelligent creation/causation can be viewed as follows:

- Creator: Sense of purpose even if it had to be that complex or precise to achieve the purpose.

Creation: It has a purpose even if it had to be that complex or precise to achieve the purpose.

- Creator: Aware of the present and past situation and vary its state and action accordingly.

Creation: Its state and action can be varied accordingly based on present and past situation.

- Creator: Recognize and use pattern or pair.

Creation: It has pattern or pair.

- Creator: Create fast.

Creation: It can be created fast.

- Creator: Control his surrounding and creation even without the will or knowledge of his surrounding/creation.

Creation: It can be controlled by its creator or by whoever its creator allows, even without its will or knowledge.

So, the intelligent creation/causation can be associated to the dice throwing, with the Artificial Intelligence (A.I.) creation as a reference, as follows:

- It has a purpose even if it had to be that complex or precise to achieve the purpose.
  - o The purpose of achieving the dice throwing result of 1,1,1,1,1,1, X is for Mr. A to recognize easily the one intelligent and powerful God.
  - o A.I is created with such complexity and precision for the purpose to serve human being.
- Its state and action can be varied accordingly based on present and past situation.
  - o The letter X of the last dice throwing result as mentioned by God to Mr. A can be varied from 1 to 6 accordingly.
  - o The A.I. can be varied and upgraded from time to time to sustain its function and/or stay relevant with various human being requirement.
- It has pattern or pair.
  - o The number 1 is repeatedly shown in the dice throwing. The scientific explanation explained a definite pattern or pair with accurate predictable outcome.
  - o There is a pattern (repeated) design applied to the A.I and the equation of science used in the design also exhibit a definite pattern or pair with accurate predictable outcome.
- It can be created fast.
  - o The number 1,1,1,1,1,1,1 is visibly thrown successively in just one round of throw and not from 279,936 rounds of trial-and-error throws.
  - o The A.I can be created by human being relatively fast.
- It can be controlled by its creator or by whoever its creator allows, even without its will or knowledge.

o The ending of the dice throwing after the 7 throws was not controlled by the dice itself, but by the dice's thrower.

o A.I. can be programmed not to cross certain limits and boundaries and can be switched on, off and controlled as-and-when required by human being, even without the will or knowledge of the A.I.

So, the dice throwing can be associated to all characters of intelligence causation/creation. So, which of the 4PEUC is more likely the intelligent entity? Can Nothing alone be that intelligent? Something alone or God alone is more likely to be that intelligent. However, the determining characteristic of intelligence, especially of the highly intelligent entity, is the following:

- Communicate clearly with other intelligent being.
  o God clearly communicated to Mr. A, claiming himself as the thrower of the dice, neither Something alone nor Nothing alone.
  o Human being communicated to A.I., its intelligent creation, claiming himself as its creator.

So, God is the possibility more likely to be true among the 4PEUC, either alone or in the entity of any possible sequence of creation between Nothing, Something and God.

What's the true sequence of creation between Nothing – Something – God? It's logical that Nothing is not likely to create Something or create God as by definition, Nothing is the absence of anything, so how could Nothing create Something or God? So, the more likely sequence of creation is between God – Something i.e., Something created God or God created Something.

16

Therefore, the 4PEUC are now reduced to <u>2 probable entities of "Ultimate Creator"</u> (2PEUC) as follows:

- God (UC) or,
- An entity of any sequence of creation between God and Something prior to the direct causation of the dice throwing, i.e.:
  o Something (UC) created God or,
  o Something (UC) created God created Something or,
  o God (UC) created Something.

Then the 2nd observer asked what if "something/somebody else" also communicated that it/he was the one that caused the dice throwing? Then Mr. A said if there were more or less, 279,936 rounds of invisible throws done simultaneously, then the thrower is more likely powerful as by definition, power is the rate of doing work. Can that "something/somebody else" be that powerful? The 2nd observer said, "What if there were more or less, 279,936 throwers?". Then Mr. A said then it was more likely to be coordinated by one being to make that one successful round of throw visible from the 279,936 (*more or less*) rounds of invisible throws. Even if there were other throwers, the powerful and intelligent one is more likely to dominate and not collaborate with all others to be self-sufficient, steer the throw to be 1,1,1,1,1,1,1 as per his owned preferred pattern, neither 2,2,2,2,2,2,2 nor 3,3,3,3,3,3,3 nor other patterns and create order to make that successful throw.

So, who/what is the UC? There was no direct observation and thus no hard evidence yet to determine the UC. Regardless of the UC, the dice throwing was more likely caused and governed by the intelligent and powerful one among the 2PEUC, so whatever/ whoever He is, He is ultimately referred as God here.

The 6th and 7th observers said, "We just don't know, we have no hard evidence".

The 6th observer said that he could not decide yet as there was no hard evidence of God. That was undecisive. The 6th observer had to decide before the time to conclude the observation (*time of no return*) expiring, otherwise the 6th observer was gambling.

The 7th observer said as there was no hard evidence, he had decided not to believe in God until proven otherwise. He said he would stick to his decision. The 7th observer was gambling as he has decided to choose a way when he don't know the truth of that chosen way and any probable ways, and his decision is not changeable till the expiry of the time to conclude the observation.

But the 6th and 7th observers argued that there was also no hard evidence that the stick and gift promised by God would also be true. Then Mr. A thought whether the texts communication by God was just a scam. What were the requirements of God for him to give the gift? Mr. A then looked back at all the text messages which basically called Mr. A to learn to believe in God, to be good to Mr. A himself and others. That seem not entirely a self-centered message but rather a caring message to Mr. A and the human species. Mr. A could also reflect how he was learning science from the 5th observer in his effort to know how God could have done it.

Even if there was no hard evidence of the gift, stick and God's existence, Mr. A could see the hard evidence of benefits in safety and health that outweigh the burden of following the requirements of God. And to be good to others is just a noble requirement.

So, Mr. A thought, "What if he was wrong in concluding God's existence?". Nothing will happen to Mr. A and yet many of the requirements of God were being done by Mr. A before receiving those text messages and proven to be beneficial that outweigh the burden. But if Mr. A is right, Mr. A will receive the gift.

Mr. A was not that too simple or lazy to finally believe in God as Mr. A had considered all the hypotheses, theory, and views from other observers.

Then the 1st observer asked Mr. A, "If the next round of throw showed a random result than rather a pattern, would Mr. A still believe in God?". Mr. A said that he could not immediately falsify God as it is still possible that the dice was thrown to get any random number for the purpose of just playing the game which made the intelligent creation/causation still possible. There was no hard evidence that the throw was not done by God. The believe of God will remain as right until proven wrong.

This dice story can be connected to many observations of this universe. Our common sense tells us that things in this universe are so complex, precise, and beautiful such that the probability that they were created randomly, by luck are logically very, very small or not likely. Can our sophisticated handphone be created just randomly, by luck even if it takes 13.8 billion years, without any intelligent creator like human being behind it?

The fine tuning of the universe also shows that the fundamental physical constants are such extraordinary precise such that if they did not, the origin and evolution of lives in the universe would not be permitted, indicating a more likely intelligent creator than rather randomness behind the creation of those precise constants for the purpose, amongst others, for lives, like us to exist.

Even if there is a simple intelligence that only aim for the survival of the fittest behind the creation of this universe 13.8 billion years ago, do you think this complex, precise and beautiful universe can exist? For example, if we ask monkeys to type continuously for 13.8 billion years, do you think we can get a Shakespeare's manuscript out of it? If we ask monkeys to flap their hands continuously for 13.8 billion years, can that monkeys change their hands to become wings and become birds? So, the question is, if not randomness or simple intelligence, who created or what caused this complex, precise and beautiful universe?

Science tells us that any living or non-living things in this universe are "made" of molecules, "made" of atoms, "made" of elementary particles. But the question is who created or what caused those elementary particles?

Science also tells us that the term "made" here can be evolution, chemical reaction, or fundamental interaction. Even if it is true, the question is who created or what caused those evolution, chemical reaction, or fundamental interaction?

Science hypotheses also tell us that the whole mechanism/equation/ law of "made" here from living/non-living things to elementary particles are called naturalism hypothesis or simultaneously happening by multiverse hypothesis or repeatedly happening by cyclic conformal cosmology hypothesis or seen as simulation hypothesis or to be all explained by the Theory of Everything. So far, they remain as hypotheses, without any hard evidence. Even if any one of the hypotheses is true, including any other new theories, the question is still who created or what caused the whole mechanism/equation/law here?

Logically, everything has a cause or creator except the beginning, the one uncaused/uncreated beginning, hereby referred as the "Ultimate Creator" (UC). Logically, the UC is necessary for anything to exist. If there is no UC, no beginning, i.e., if there is an endless, infinite chains of cause/creator, then logically, anything will not exist, as the chains must end somewhere or there must be a finite number of chains of cause/creator. In other words, there must be a beginning for anything to exist.

> Note: The beginning here also include thing with eternal existence (no start, no end) as if it's true that there is no space, no time before/outside this universe, the word beginning can be misleading.

Where did the chains of cause/creator end or simply, where did it begin? The end of the causation chains can be shorter than the end of the creation chains. How? An event can be caused by the thing (X) without other thing caused X to cause that event (i.e., causation end at X) but X can still be created by other thing. E.g., we can cause something by our own freewill without others causing us to cause that something, but we are created by our parents, by our grandparents, by molecules, by atoms, by elementary particles and so on. So, logically, the ultimate ending of these causation/creation chains must be at the <u>one indivisible entity, that cannot be further divided, that cannot be further created by other thing</u>, the one uncaused/uncreated beginning, hereby referred as the one UC.

If in the beginning, the UC is one and nothing else, then how could it then create varieties of things? Less likely, it created things from nothing but more likely, from part of itself. How? Just like matter is known to self-replicate to form varieties of matter in this universe such as biological cells *(living thing)* and crystal *(non-living thing)*. Even a computer program, Worm, can replicate itself as a malware computer program to spread to other computers. And matter can replicate to form varieties of matter such as by mutation due to DNA replication error. Identical matter can also form varieties of matter when combined in various multiple forms. For example, on how proton formed variety of chemical elements; when one, it becomes Hydrogen, when two, it becomes Helium, when three, it becomes Lithium, when four, it becomes Beryllium and so on and on, with each chemical element having its own variation of characteristics.

Even if this one UC can form a cycle such as its own creation/causation feeding back anything relevant to the UC, the existence of this one UC is still necessary in the first place for the cycle to exist.

If there is a claim of multiple different UCs, then that UCs are not the UC as that UCs did not create/cause each other UCs, therefore did not create everything.

Even if there are actually multiple different UCs, these UCs will more likely, ultimately, cause/create under one UC. Just like a scenario of multiple, different people interacting. They may initially act by their own way, but when their acts adversely affect each other, they will either act based on consensus i.e., based on common understanding/agreement as influenced by the <u>one</u> influencing people or in case of conflict among them, if the conflict getting worst with no consensus, ultimately the act will be dominated by the <u>one</u> people that won the conflict, either by force or not.

Therefore, the UC is ultimately and logically one.

Even if it happens that the creation is actually dominating its UC, that creation has become the UC as the dominated UC is being actively owned by its creation. Just like a Tesla car. Although Tesla was co-founded by Martin Eberhard and Marc Tarpenning in 2003 and the car is directly manufactured by the workers of Tesla, we simply but rightfully say that Tesla car is now created by Elon Musk, the largest shareholder/owner, and active CEO of Tesla since 2008.

Can nature be considered the UC? It depends on which angle we are looking at. By definition, nature is all things not made by people. Since UC is not made by people, therefore UC can be classified as nature. However, by function, UC is not equal to its creation, so since its creation are nature and UC is not equal to its creation, therefore UC is not nature.

To recap, the UC is either one of the following mutually exclusive and exhaustive <u>4 possible entities of "Ultimate Creator"</u> (4PEUC), i.e.:

- Nothing (UC),
- Something (UC),
- God (UC),

- An entity of any possible sequence of creation between Nothing, Something and God, such as:
  o Nothing (UC) created Something,
  o Nothing (UC) created God,
  o Something (UC) created God,
  o God (UC) created Something,
  o Something (UC) created God created Something,
  o Nothing (UC) created Something created God,
  o Nothing (UC) created God created Something,
  o Nothing (UC) created Something created God created Something.

Note:

1. *Something can be singular or multiple sequence of creation of variations of something, e.g., Something1 created Something2 created Something3, etc.*
2. *Entity is thing with independent and distinct existence.*

Many things in this universe can be scientifically observed as fundamentally created by elementary particles and fundamentally caused by evolution, chemical reaction and/or fundamental interaction.

So, the true entity among the 4PEUC is more likely to be intelligent than rather non-intelligent as characteristics of intelligent creation/causation can be associated to the fundamental creation and fundamental causation of the universe as follows:

- It has a purpose even if it had to be that complex or precise to achieve the purpose.

- o Elementary particles: To be the smallest building blocks of the universe.
- o Evolution: To change the characteristic of the species.
- o Chemical reaction: To transform one set of chemical substances to another.
- o Fundamental interaction: To govern how objects or particles interact and how certain particles decay.
- Its state and action can be varied accordingly based on present and past situation.
  - o Elementary particles: It varies into 17 elementary particles as per the Standard Model. Charm mesons can change into their antiparticle and back again as discovered by Oxford researchers at CERN.
  - o Evolution: It varies as mutation, genetic drift, gene flow, non-random mating, and natural selection.
  - o Chemical reaction: It varies as combination, decomposition, displacement, or precipitation reaction.
  - o Fundamental interaction: It varies from one super force to gravitational, electromagnetic, weak, and strong nuclear forces.
- It has pattern or pair.
  - o Elementary particles: There are pairs of matter - anti matter particles, up - down quarks, top - bottom quarks, mass - massless particles, matter - force particles.
  - o Evolution: It has pattern of divergent, parallel, and convergent evolution.
  - o Chemical reaction: Chemical equation explained a definite pattern or pair with accurate predictable outcome There are pairs of exothermic – endothermic reaction, increasing – decreasing disorder reaction.

- o Fundamental interaction: Equation of Physics explained a definite pattern or pair with accurate predictable outcome. There are pairs of variables – constant, space – time, static – motion, gravitational-electromagnetic force (*effects can be seen in everyday life*) and strong – weak nuclear forces (*produce forces at minuscule, subatomic distances*)
- It can be created fast.
  - o Elementary particles: Created within 10^{-36} second after the Big Bang.
  - o Evolution: It can start to happen relatively fast after abiogenesis.
  - o Chemical reaction: Spontaneous chemical reaction can be created by exothermic and increasing disorder reaction.
  - o Fundamental interaction: Created as one super force within 10^{-43} second after the Big Bang.
- It can be controlled by its creator or by whoever its creator allows, even without its will or knowledge.
  - o Elementary particles: Human can use and control elementary particles to his benefits in medicine (*cancer therapy, diagnostic instrumentation*), monitor nuclear waste nonproliferation, power transmission, biomedicine, and drug development, understanding turbulence and computing (*world wide web and the Grid*)
  - o Evolution: Human activities can influence and control evolution such as causing declines in species population by global warming, habitat loss from agricultural activities, deforestation, urbanization, hunting, fishing,

26

degrading ecosystems especially soil, water, air by pollution and waste and disrupting species interaction.

o Chemical reaction: Human can use and control chemical reaction to his benefit e.g., adding reaction inhibitor or catalyst to decrease or increase respectively the rate of a chemical reaction.

o Fundamental interaction: Human can overcome gravity, use, and control nuclear forces and electromagnetic forces to his benefit.

So, the fundamental creation/causation of this universe can be associated to all characters of intelligent causation/creation. Which of the 4PEUC is more likely the intelligent entity? Can Nothing alone be that intelligent? Although Something alone or God alone can be associated with the characteristics of intelligence, Something alone or Nothing alone clearly fails one determining characteristic of intelligence, especially of the highly intelligent entity i.e., communicate clearly with other intelligent being.

Only God communicate clearly with human being (*through God's revelation, through God's Angel, through God's Messenger or through inspiration*), claiming Himself as the creator of this universe, neither Something alone nor Nothing alone. If anyone/anything, claim itself as God, we will take that anyone/anything as possibly God here, not as Something for sake of classifying, for ease of understanding. God is more likely to have communicated with human being from Day 1 human being on Earth as logically, any intelligent creator will communicate to its intelligent creation as soon as the first one is alive. So, whoever claiming himself as God, the creator of this universe and have communicated to the first human being on earth are the possible candidates of God, to be further explained afterwards. But for now, the more likely possibility to be true among the 4PEUC is either God alone or an entity of any possible sequence of creation between Nothing – Something – God.

What's the true sequence of creation between Nothing – Something – God? Logically, Nothing is not likely to create Something or create God as by definition, Nothing is the absence of anything, so how could Nothing create Something or magically create God?

Nothingness means no particles or antiparticles, no matter or radiation and no identifiable quanta of any type. Even a vacuum of space contains something i.e., particles, gases, radiation, quanta, etc. There is no such thing as nothingness in this universe. Everything is something.

Even if Nothing really exist and this Nothing really create Something or God, it is meaningless to say the UC is Nothing i.e., meaningless to appreciate, respect, serve, obey, or do anything to Nothing (*the UC*) and it only give meaning only when we do same with Something or God that Nothing presumably created. Likewise, it is also meaningless to say Something create Nothing. Just like it will become meaningless when we say we do nothing, and it only gives meaning only when we say we do something about it. So, the more likely and meaningful sequence of creation is between God – Something i.e., Something created God or God created Something.

Therefore, the 4PEUC are now reduced to 2 probable entities of "Ultimate Creator" (2PEUC) as follows:

- God (UC) or,
- An entity of any sequence of creation between God and Something prior to the direct creation of the fundamental creation/causation, i.e.:
  o Something (UC) created God or,
  o Something (UC) created God created Something or,
  o God (UC) created Something.

The level of knowledge and intelligence of the Entity is less likely constant but more likely constantly growing over time and adequate during the creation of the elementary particles and universal laws to create the universe to be as it is.

Apart from intelligent, it is also more likely that the Entity is so powerful to enable simultaneous and countless energetic events in the universe. Powerful here is regardless of whether the Entity itself is that powerful and/or its creation are powerful. Just like we can consider man as powerful as long as he dominates his created powerful tools, machineries, system or team.

The Entity is also more likely to be One or dominated by the One (*if the Entity consist of multiple things*) to rightfully coordinate that overall simultaneous events in the universe. Even if those events can be self-driven/organized by design of that creation/causation, higher intervention from the One Entity will still be required to address any emerging anomalies and changes. And if there are conflicts among its creation, it can be effectively resolved by the One Entity having the intelligence and power to overrule or dominate all its creation. Resolved here don't necessarily mean resolved as deemed right by the creation but to the greater good as deemed right by the

One Entity. Therefore, the One Entity is more likely for such overall and sustained order in this universe.

And the intelligent, powerful one is also more likely to dominate than to collaborate with all others, including its competitors, if any to be self-sufficient and steering to its owned preferred pattern and direction, either within the Entity itself (*if Entity consist of multiple things*) or to His creation.

So, what's/who's actually the one "Ultimate Creator" (UC) among the 2PEUC? We don't know yet the answer for certain as we have no hard evidence. The UC is currently beyond the reach of science. But we cannot just stop questioning and answering here just because science don't know. We can't wait for science to know the UC as our life on earth is limited. Our "don't know" is also everywhere, even in things that we think we know. We use common sense to infer logically if we can't get the hard evidence or science to know things for certain or re-define the question to move forward.

Whether the UC is:

- God (*i.e., God is the uncreated/uncaused beginning that created "all things", that created this universe*) or,
- An entity of any sequence of creation between God and Something, either:
  o Something as UC created God then created this universe or,
  o Something as UC created God then created Something then created this Universe or,

o Something as UC created this universe partially then created God then created/shaped this universe completely or,

o God as UC created Something then created this universe.

The question that ultimately matter is the following:

- Regardless of the actual UC, is the intelligent and powerful one exists among the 2PEUC that dominate "all things" (*all elementary particles, evolution, chemical reaction, gravity, electromagnetic force, weak and strong nuclear forces, scientific and universal laws and orders, atoms, molecules, living and non-living things in this universe*), including dominating the UC itself if it is not the UC?

The answer is more likely "yes", and the reasons can be summarized as follows:

- The intelligent creator among the 2PEUC is more likely to exist as "all things" are more likely to exhibit intelligent creation/causation as demonstrated by the fundamental creation (*elementary particles*) and fundamental causation (*evolution, chemical reaction, and fundamental interaction*) of this universe.
- That intelligent creator is also more likely so powerful and one such that He governs "all things" in this universe to such sustained order, simply dominating "all things" to such effective pattern and direction, such that certainly, human being still existing and progressing till now.

Whatever/whoever dominate "all things" (*including dominating the UC if it is not the UC*) is ultimately referred as God here, even if God could be Something initially. So, regarding the 2PEUC:

- God is the UC in one probable entity and,
- In another probable entity, God is more likely dominating the UC (*Something*) or the UC (*Something*) is acting like God, more likely dominating all others.

Therefore, back to the question of the one UC, the answer can be concluded that <u>the "Ultimate Creator" (UC) is more likely God in whichever probable entity of the UC.</u> So, being the "Ultimate Creator", God created "all things", created and govern this universe.

As God is intelligent, He communicates to His creation, including us. Whoever/whatever that did not communicate to us, not claiming itself as God, not claiming itself as the Creator of "all things", regardless of its presumed greatness in intelligence or power, is not considered as God but as Something here. Even if anyone/anything claim itself as God, we will take that anyone/anything as possible candidate of God here. Just like when we create A.I., we communicate to A.I., claiming ourselves as its creator. Then it's up to us to decide whether the claimant is God or not.

Who has claimed himself as God? There were many stories of claimants but the one that matter to us are those stories during the time of the first human being on earth as any intelligent creator, logically will communicate to its intelligent creation as soon as the first one is alive. Among those claimants are commonly known as "Ancient Gods" or some believe as aliens. They demonstrated their intelligence and power by demonstrating their advanced knowledge and technologies capable of high - speed travel, complex/precision construction, mass destruction, in-penetrable self- defense, etc., controlling their competitors including human being. So, can we consider that "Ancient Gods" or aliens as God? Then, we should ask:

- As God dominates "all things" (*all elementary particles, etc., etc.......living and non-living things in this universe*) such that God control them even without their will or knowledge, then <u>why all those troubles</u> by the "Ancient Gods"/aliens to:
  o Show themselves up,
  o Demonstrate their advanced technological products to demonstrate their intelligence and power,
  o Defend and protect themselves from being harmed by their owned creation?

  This just clearly demonstrate the <u>lack of undisputed dominance of the "Ancient Gods"/aliens over their presumed owned creation</u>. When human being created A.I., he just simply uses his switch to dominate his A.I. Likewise, when God intend a thing, it just happen as per God's revelation in Appendix A:3. When human being created A.I., the A.I is programmed to recognize us as its creator. Just like we have an innate (*inborn, natural*) thinking that there is a Creator when we see this universe although our freewill will then allow us to believe or not to believe in the Creator.

- How could we have more than one God?
- Do that "Ancient Gods"/aliens have one big boss or someone that it serves or its Creator? God's revelations tell us of the

existence of God's creation before human being such as angels, devils, jinn, etc.

You may ask, "*If there is an intelligent God, how do we explain some of the random and chaotic nature of the universe?*" It is because we have yet to know its purpose for such randomness. It's like the electron which has a kind of probabilistic existence, being in all possible places and doing all possible things at all possible times as per the Heisenberg uncertainty principle. With this randomness, we only know recently that electron is an elementary particle which has the purpose to be among the smallest building blocks of the universe, participating in chemical reactions and can be utilized for power transmission in the form of electricity, to obtain high resolution images of biological/non-biological specimen by electron microscopy, etc. And if those parts of the universe which are random/chaotic but made up of elementary particles which exhibit intelligent creation/causation, then how do we know it's not that those parts of the universe are also the intelligent creation/causation?

Similarly, "*If God dominate "all things", why are there devil, why are there bad immoral conduct happening in seemingly uncontrolled manner?*" Domination can be direct and indirect (*and the former is not necessarily stronger than the latter*). Although some of us may think that they <u>directly</u> dominate themselves as they can do whatever they want as per their freewill, but actually, some of us just can't resist their evil will, as devil has <u>indirectly</u> dominated them to make happen their evil will. However, how do you know it's not that God <u>indirectly</u> dominate in the bigger context, by allowing it to happen as per their freewill to such extent for the purpose of the greater good? Further explanation on God's creation rules and the greater good will be given in the next questions and answers.

You may also ask, *"Can the elementary particles be the UC?"*. Well, we don't know whether the known elementary particles created everything in the universe as the composition of the Dark Matter and Dark Energy is still unknown. But we do know that there are purposes like any other intelligent creation/causation, i.e., either the purpose of Dark Matter is to provide the gravitational effect that help in the formation of galaxies, or there is no Dark Matter, and the effect is instead, caused by gravity itself (*probable new discovery of other mechanism/purpose of the gravity*). As for Dark Energy, either its purpose is to expand the universe or there is no Dark Energy, and the expansion is instead, caused by the vacuum energy of the black holes (*probable new discovery of other purpose of black holes*). Given the time, I believe, we will know much more later about Dark Energy, Dark Matter, gravity and blackholes such that they can also be associated with the intelligent creation/causation like all other things in this universe.

"If the elementary particles are found later to also created the Dark Matter/Energy or any other things, can the elementary particles be the UC and be considered as God?". Well, they did not communicate to us, claiming themselves as God but instead, they can be controlled by human being.

"If so, can there be no God and that the elementary particles are just the uncaused/uncreated beginning, the UC?". But the UC is one, the elementary particles are not one and comprise of multiple different particles. Even if later, we discover one UC particle that created all existing elementary particles, but how are "all things" governed to

such sustained order that demonstrate the existence of the intelligent and powerful one? *"All things are governed by the universal laws of fundamental interaction, chemical reaction and evolution"*. But laws without the enforcer, will not cause the effect. Just like if there are criminal laws without the police and judge that enforce the laws, criminals will go on unpunished. *"But these universal laws are self-existence, self-enforcing and evolving over time"*. And that also sound to mean the universal laws are also the UC, but the UC is one, not multiple different UCs (*UC particle and UC laws*). Furthermore, the universal laws are not one and comprise of multiple laws and within one law, there are multiple states and patterns. Even if later science will discover the one Theory of Everything to explain how this universe is governed, that one theory will be an integrated theories of variables (*matter, forces, etc.*) and constants, which in reality is not one.

Even if we believe that the one Theory of Everything can explain the one UC particle, can explain the governing of this universe and self-enforcing like the one entity of UC with its integrated nature (*of matter, forces, constants, etc.*), the believe of this one Theory is like believing in the intelligent and powerful one that dominate "all things", ultimately referred as God here. So why wait that long for the evidence of God's existence or non-existence by this one Theory of Everything and not use this logical inference to believe in God now?

Even if you have made up your mind that there is no God now and then, there is no Ultimate Creator, how do you know it's not that in the far future, there will be more likely an Ultimate Creation, a being pursuing to dominate "all things" with its super intelligence/power derived from the accelerating technological advancement that we witness now and with such technological capability, that being has time-travelled back to our time and before our time, leaving behind signs that we see as God now?

So, in either way of looking back in time or forward in time, God's existence is more likely than God's non-existence. Those who still insisted "we just don't know" despite this logic, is either dishonest to himself or having a tight closed mind about the word God.

You may also argue that "*As there are so many <u>more-likely</u> scenarios for God's existence that mathematically, the resultant probability of those multiplied probabilities is <u>less-likely</u>*". But equitably with so many <u>less-likely</u> scenarios for God's non-existence, the resultant probability is <u>unlikely</u> (*lower than less likely*)". Still, we have relatively higher probability of truth for God's existence than to God's non-existence.

So, I believe in God as the probability of God's existence is higher than the probability of God non-existence. The believe in God also does not require evidence as by definition, it cannot be proved or disproved. And there are net benefits in believing in God. If I am wrong in my decision to believe in God, I just rest in peace after death and yet by following God's commands, I can live safely and healthily with self-actualization of being giving (*to be further explained in next questions and answers*), though with limited freedom/joy/pleasure, that outweigh the burden in believing in God and outweigh the opportunity losses of the unlimited freedom/joy/ pleasure in my lifetime. But if I am right, Heaven awaits me.

On the other hand, if I am non-believer of God, I will rest in peace after death with unlimited joy/pleasure during my lifetime, if I am right. But if I am wrong, I will be eternally in Hell frying. So, there is no net benefit if I am wrong.

Some non-believers of God believe that God is actually devil (*we have been tricked, we are just devil's slaves in this world, there is no Hell, no Heaven after death*) and that we, ourselves are actually God. Even if this absurdity is actually true, the same logic still applies, i.e., if I am actually wrong (*that God is actually devil*), I will still rest in peace after death (*as there are no Hell, no Heaven*) and yet by following God's commands, I can live safely and healthily in this world, learning and giving for the well-being of human being. But if I am right, Heaven awaits me.

So, I am right to believe in God until proven wrong.

Q7: Do you think non-believers of God will accept your logic and science to believe in God?

A: It's like when someone is so used to use pen to sketch. He will likely refuse to use pencil to sketch. He also will likely to over-use the pen to rub his itching back. If the pen is conscious, the pen is likely to misuse him to glorify the pen as a sketching God.

As long as he doesn't want to open his mind to use the pencil, he will never use the pencil. As long as he doesn't want to open his mind to use the pen and pencil as a pair working together to get the best of the two worlds, he won't move further to improve his sketching world.

There are five groups of non-believers of God. The First Group is the "evidence" (*"We just don't know"*) group while the Second Group is the "freedom" (*"We don't know much, I don't care"*) group. The Third Group is the "comfortable" (*"We don't want to know, I'm OK now"*) group, the Fourth group is the "open mind" (*"I don't know, tell me now"*) group and the Fifth Group is the "frustrated" (*"Now I don't know what to believe"*) group.

The First Group is typically the hard-core people of science who demand absolute truth by scientific theories or hypothesis with observable/testable evidence only. However, in making their scientific theories right, they don't mind adding up assumption and unknown factor in their theories to align with the observation made and called this unknown factor by any name provided it is not God factor. Example is the unknown Dark Energy and Dark Matter which constitute 95% of the universe and the source of the fundamental physical constants.

They refuse to accept logic to believe in God although science is just a branch of logic to give good reason to believe, as they want absolute truth only by scientific evidence. They don't mind researching further to explain all the scientific theories such as looking for the Theory of Everything provided their answer is not God. Giving the answer as God is deemed a too simple or lazy approach to explain this universe although they still need to answer later the source of the Theory of Everything should they discover it later.

They don't mind that the accuracy and validity of science can change over time as science is deemed progressive and proven to work. When discussing about God, they will not just accept scientific hypothesis as inference to God, they can only accept testable/observable scientific hypothesis which can never be established in explaining God, as there cannot be any observable/ testable evidence of God's existence. When questioned about God, the standard answer is "There is no evidence. We just don't know". However, they themselves don't mind using unproven scientific hypothesis and logical inference to decide in their day-to-day life.

The Second Group put utmost priority to freedom of life, fulfilment of desire and to be fully in-charge of their own life. They reject any being or belief system that limit their freedom of life, freedom to do what they like to do, especially if that being or belief system has no direct authority on them.

Just like vegetables, despite that we know that there is hard evidence that vegetables are good for our health, but some of us still reject eating vegetables as vegetables taste not to their liking. Just like drug, despite that it is proven bad for our health with strictest law on drug enforced, but some of us still abuse drug as it tastes to their liking and won't bother of that restricting law.

If they can even reject things which have hard evidence of benefit or accept things which are proven endangering them, you can imagine their rejection to God that limit their freedom with no hard evidence of existence.

They rely heavily on the First Group to defend their position. Sometimes, they create their own belief system or follow any belief system that is based on freedom of life, provided it is not God. As long as there are crowds or followers in the First or Second Group, they tend to follow the crowds partially blindly. When dealing with question of God, they too demand hard evidence but not hesitate to use logical inference method to decide in their day-to-day life. When they can't defend their point about God, the standard answer is, "We don't know much, I don't care".

The Third group was born and brought up by parents or live in families who are non-believers of God, feel comfortable that way, resistant to any change that are deemed burdening or won't dare to go against their parents/families. They too rely heavily on the First Group to defend their position. If topic of God is initiated, they will tell themselves, "I don't want to know, I'm OK now".

So, as long as they don't want to open their minds, they will not accept my logic and science to believe in God. Their disbelieving of God become even stronger when they have the characters of the First, Second or Third Group combined.

The Fourth Group, on the other hand, is open minded and likely to accept my logic and science.

The Fifth Group is the frustrated group who were once believers of God but later become non-believers of God when it seems God did not help them upon their plea for help during their suffering or bad times despite their obedience to God's commands. When hearing stories about God, the standard remark is "Now I don't know what to believe". For this group, I humbly advise to re-open their mind about God and consider my explanation of God's action in later stages of this question-and-answer session.

Q8: Why do some non-believers of God don't want to open their minds and what's your view?

A: It's the ego and the tendency to look only for what's wrong in what they don't like after achieving certain status of always being right (*either truly or perceived*).

"Why should I believe in this medieval man fairy tale stories, telling me how to live my life, stopping me from doing what I like to do that's proven OK to me so far and burdening me unnecessarily"?

It's like someone having a preconceived opinion about something and jump to the gun to conclude negatively about the thing. It's like someone hearing a story from his friend who claimed to hear stories from Tourist A saying that a Place C was messy, and Tourist B was telling that Place C was smelly and immediately jump to the gun to claim that what they saw was rubbish, so the country is dirty due to the moving-backward government.

We can ask the following questions about his claims of the event, the effect and the cause to help him open his mind.

What exactly do he mean by messy, smelly, rubbish (*the events*), dirty country (*the effect*) and moving-backward government (*the cause*)? Where, when, how much/many exactly?

How do he know it's true? Is the claim:

- Direct observation or indirect from trustable/reliable source? It's like saying:

- o Toyota has similar parts like Jaguar, so Toyota come from Jaguar.
- o Seeing the car engine and telling the car interior must be likewise.
- o Engine telling the tires that the engine is the one that move the car and denying that man design, operate and maintain the car to move there and then.
- o Although car alarm is communicating the engine temperature is high, the fuel is instead believed to be low.
- o Something imaginary after playing too many cars video games.
- Consistent with another claim? One saying messy, the other one saying smelly? Which is which? It's like one saying Jaguar is a car, the other one saying Jaguar is an animal.
- Directly caused by the claim? If it's due to the government is moving-backward (*the cause*), then why is the rubbish (*the event*) not happening at other time/location/quantity, when/where the moving-backward government (*the cause*) can happen? If it's due to the rubbish (*the event*), then why is the dirtiness (*the effect*) not happening at other time/location, when/where the rubbish (*the event*) can happen?
- Directly caused by that claim alone? Is the moving-backward government the only possible cause of rubbish? Is the rubbish the only possible cause of dirtiness? It's like saying "car color is different, so the car engine will break down".

How do he know it's Not that:

- It was a <u>temporary</u> smell due to painting work and temporary mess due to housekeeping to be done only after

43

work completion for the <u>permanent</u> decoration of the work area?

- The told stories by the tourists were just their <u>metaphor or analogy or allegory</u> than rather to be taken <u>literally</u> as dirty, messy, and smelly to make the story meaningful? It's like when told to go straight to the roundabout, the car driver took it literally to go straight crossing the roundabout.

- Even if it was rubbish, they were standing inside a rubbish dump yard, a <u>small</u> fraction of a <u>big</u> clean country that contained the rubbish with due regard to safety, health, and environment? It's like saying "Going to the star by not stopping the car".

- Even if it was rubbish, it was an improvement opportunity for the rubbish, a <u>non-useful product</u> to be recycled and processed into safe and <u>useful products</u> for this moving-forward government?

- Even if it was rubbish, it was an improvement opportunity for the finding of the rubbish to be taken as <u>proactive</u> feedback for this moving-forward government to take <u>reactive</u> act to avoid further escalation of rubbish generation?

- Even if it was rubbish, it was an improvement opportunity for <u>jobs creation</u> in the rubbish collection and recycling <u>works</u> for this moving-forward government?

- Even if it was rubbish, if he would <u>extend his view beyond</u> this country and further in the <u>past,</u> he will be finding:

  o the cause or source of the rubbish was coming from his own country?

  o more rubbish in his own country, swept in carpets or package to look nice?

o It's like "bicycle complaining the car is slow moving".

- He is actually scared to be called the traitor by his own group if he is supporting that group classified "moving-backward" country, for going against his own group?

If the above questions are not effective, my answer is, "Let action speaks louder than words to continually be closer to the truth, taking opportunities of the safety and health benefit".

Stop closing his mind about God and make a start. Start to prioritize on one easy doing, quick gaining God's command that relate to safety and health, later the hard doing, slow gaining ones. Start to inquire on that God's command, who can help, as a common pre-step regardless of the main step of doing it or not or which option to choose. If later decided, start to move it progressively and observe if there is any quick gain, later one big move. Start to prepare to open more of his mind to God and God's command if it is proven to yield quick gain, ready to execute as and when required.

By opening his mind about God, he is more likely to be closer to the truth about God. Later, he should then open his heart about God. This opening of heart is called faith. Faith is the belief based on conviction, not on evidence. Conviction is a firmly held belief. This conviction arises after he started to realize the truth from all the starts mentioned previously but these starts can only happen if he first open or re-open his mind about God. Conviction allows him to overcome any obstacle to move further forward as he has a firmly held belief in what he is doing. Without conviction, any obstacle can quickly become a permanent barrier to know better the truth about God.

I also believe that eventually there will still be some non-believers of God regardless of how logical or scientific the explanation of God's existence can be, once the mind is shut closed tight. Ironically, that will also keep the opposite pair of believers and non-believers of God to prevail for the greater good.

Q9: If God exist, how do you think God governs this universe and what is the purpose for existence of human being?

A: God governs this universe by God's rules such as the creation rule of pairs as per God's revelation in Appendix A:11 and continual testing as per Appendix A:44, for the greater good.

A pair is interdependent to perform, sustain or vary its function accordingly. Pairs can be opposite and non-opposite. Examples of opposite pair are male-female, electron-proton. Non-opposite pair can be identical pair and non-identical pair. Examples of identical pairs are Hydrogen molecule, H^2, Nitrogen molecule, N^2. There are also identical pairs of 2,3,4, up to 116,117,118 of proton to make the chemical element Helium, Lithium, Beryllium up to Livermorium, Tennessine, Oganesson respectively. Example of non-identical pair is animal-plant. Animal inhales oxygen from the air and exhales carbon dioxide. Plant takes in carbon dioxide and releases oxygen back into the air.

A circle exhibit pairs such as left-right, top-down, start-end. So do a cycle, and we can see how a cycle is manifesting in the life of plant, animal, human being, planets, stars, etc.

Opposite pairs, when utilized in the right mixture, phase or alternation based on selected time, space or condition can produce net benefit such that the pros of the two extremes can be harnessed and synergized whilst the cons of the two extremes can be mitigated, for continual improvement and progress.

Just like the opposite pair of good – bad:

- Continual challenge by the bad with quick-forming perception and strong impact of the bad will drives the good to be continually improved to be greater than good. Just like the political opposition party continually challenging the ruling party, using the media to twist good vision/strategy/plan as bad ones, amplifying, and sensationalizing any news of flawed, bad implementation that will drive the ruling party to continually improve itself.
- Bad can be bad in smaller context but can be good in bigger context, for the greater good. Just like sacrificial anodes, these smaller, inexpensive anodes are susceptible to bad corrosion but can be good, preventing corrosion to the bigger, expensive equipment.
- Bad can be bad in isolation but can be good in combination. Just like drug, in isolation, it is bad, damaging health but combined with good doctors' prescription, it becomes good, healing for health.
- Good and bad, learning from each other to be better. Just like a rich person can learn how the poor person save money for the rich person to be richer. On the other hand, the poor person can also learn how the rich person strategize and implement his financial/economic plan for the poor person to be rich.

Human being emulated, (*consciously or not*), the concept of pair in their creation such as bolt - nut, male - female coupler, lock - key, scissors, symmetrical design, customer - supplier, main - backup system, vision - mission, strategy - plan, leader - followers, PDCA (*plan-do-check-action*) cycle, risk - reward, etc.

So, how do you know it's not that the creation rule of pair is forming the basis of law of sciences and other universal orders as (*or will be*) discovered by human being?

Another God's rule is the rule of continual testing. I think, with such rule, proactive, relevant feedback can be obtained, providing opportunities for appropriate reactive act to avoid (*or prevent escalation of*) negative outcome or promote positive outcome, to persevere patiently (*as per God's revelation in Appendix A:44*), for continual improvement and progress in the future. However, if despite this proactive feedback, inappropriate reactive act is still done, then there will be consequence to be borne.

The advance notice of continual testing through God's revelations will also prompt us to continually be in prepared mode, to efficiently and effectively, execute works to mitigate any potential threats and seize potential opportunities in our life before and after death.

Human being emulated, (*consciously or not*), the concept of continual testing in their design, construction, operation, and maintenance of their creation (*product, material, services, system, etc.*), as a relevant, proactive feedback to give opportunities for appropriate reactive act to assure the final successful outcome with associated rewards. Those reacting inappropriately to the feedback from this testing will be "dealt with", including giving further chance to learn and recover and if the inappropriate reaction persists, they will be somehow penalized for any final unsuccessful outcome.

The purpose for human being existence is to serve God by obeying God's commands such that human being will continually be safe, healthy, learning and giving for the well-being of human being until their destined death for continued survival of human species for the greater good and be rewarded in Heaven for such obedience.

The greater good, to me, is continual improvement and progress that are relevant to God and God's selected creation and other greatness that only God know.

These are just my inferences from God's revelations (*refer Appendix A:19 - 26, A:42 - 43*), only God know the absolute truth.

Q10: So, you infer that the laws of sciences were created by God. Please explain.

A: God told us of the pairs.

I can infer that the laws and equations of physics are based on God's rule of pairs, i.e., the opposite pairs of constants - variables and within the variables are the opposite pair of static – motion and non-identical pair of space - time.

The first law of physics state "an object (*static*) will not change its motion (*motion*) unless a force acts on it".

The second law of physics state "the force of an object is equal to its mass (*static*) time its acceleration (*motion*) ".

The third law of physic state "when two object interact, they apply forces to each other of equal magnitude and <u>opposite</u> direction".

Newton equation of gravitational force, $F = Gm1m2/d^2$ can be seen as:

$F = \mathbf{G}$ (*constant*) $\mathbf{m1m2/d^2}$ (*variables*)
$m1\ g = G\ m1m2/d^2$
$g = Gm2/d^2$
$9.8\ m/s^2 = Gm2/\ d^2$
$\mathbf{9.8\ m/s^2}$ (*motion*) $= \mathbf{Gm2}$ (*static*)$/\ d^2$
$9.8\ m/\underline{s^2}$ (*time*) $= Gm2/\ \mathbf{\underline{d}^2}$ (*space*)

Einstein equation of energy, $E= mc^2$ can be seen as;
$E = \mathbf{\underline{m}}$(*variable*) $\underline{\mathbf{c}}^2$ (*constant*)

I can also infer that the laws and equations of chemistry are also based on God's rule of pairs, i.e., <u>the opposite pair of endothermic – exothermic reaction</u> and <u>identical pair of atoms in the reactant and product</u> (*i.e., identical number of atoms in the reactant and product as per the law of chemistry*), for example, the photosynthesis in the plant and metabolism in human being.

Endothermic reaction: Heat is absorbed.

    Reactant   Product

$6CO_2 + 6H_2O + heat = C_6H_{12}O_6 + 6O_2$

In photosynthesis, the carbon dioxide (CO_2) and water (H_2O) taken by the plant are converted by the light (heat) energy captured by chlorophyll into carbohydrate ($C_6H_{12}O_6$) and release oxygen (O_2) into the air.

In the reactant, there are 6 (C) carbon atoms, 12 hydrogen (H) atoms and 18 oxygen (O) atoms and there are <u>identical number of atoms</u> in the product.

Exothermic reaction: Heat is released.

In metabolism, human being takes carbohydrate ($C_6H_{12}O_6$) and breathe in oxygen (O_2) from the air and produce energy (heat), water (H_2O) and breathe out carbon dioxide (CO_2) back into the air.

    Reactant   Product

$C_6H_{12}O_6 + 6O_2 = heat + 6H_2O + 6CO_2$

In the reactant, there are 6 (C) carbon atoms, 12 hydrogen (H) atoms and 18 oxygen (O) atoms and there are <u>identical number of atoms</u> in the product.

Numerous other laws and equations of physic and chemistry can be seen as having pairs.

No doubt that human invented mathematics, but it is meant to discover the scientific law as created by God.

The rule of pairs also enables us to challenge the truth of any law or theory without any pair, e.g. third law of biology which state all living organisms arose in an evolutionary process.

It states "all" instead of "all with the exception". It states evolution, instead of evolution with the other non-evolution process.

You may ask, "But the law and equation of science is more detailed than those pairs, why should we believe it's created by God?". I believe, God provide the guide for acquiring knowledge (*e.g., these pairs of his creation*) and not spoon feed human with detailed knowledge such that human will continually use and develop his God's given great mind, be learning, and giving for the well-being of human being.

These are just my inferences to God's revelation and scientific truth, only God know the absolute truth.

Q11: If God is so intelligent and powerful, why God took that long 13.8 billion years to create this universe and human being?

A: How do you know it's not that God experiences so short a time but human being experiences so long a time to appreciate and emulate God's intelligence and power?

How do you know it's not that God choose that pairs as the rule of God's creation, i.e., the pairs of earth time - universal time, creation – evolution for the greater good?

After the Big Bang, it took 13.8 billion years <u>earth time</u> to create this universe and human being. If the scientific hypothesis of no space and no time before the Big Bang is true and if God is outside this universe, then God experience no time <u>(*universal time*)</u> to create this universe and human being. And according to Einstein Theory of Relativity, time is slower in high-speed travel or high-gravity space. So, if God is inside the universe and if God must be everywhere, every time, including in high-gravity space in this vast universe, then he must travel so fast to that so high-gravity space such that God will experience so short a time <u>(*universal time*)</u>.

Human should appreciate how God did it; from God's <u>creation</u> of the elementary particles and law of physic and chemistry that caused <u>evolution</u> of the elementary particles to become atom, molecules, stella nebula, star, black hole, planets and then <u>creation</u> of life from non-life organisms by abiogenesis with law of biology to cause <u>evolution</u> to variety of plants and animals and later <u>creation</u> of human being with that distinct chromosome no. 2 to be that intelligent, distinct from other lives.

Consciously or not, human emulated on how God did it when human created A.I. which started with the <u>creation</u> of tool, then <u>evolution</u> to variety of tool and machine and then <u>creation</u> of computer program to automate the machine, then <u>evolution</u> to variety of automated machines, then later <u>creation</u> of A.I. that are programmed to think rationally like human being and predictably,

<u>evolution</u> to variety of A.I. in the future and the cycle (*pair*) of creation – evolution go on and on.

These are just my inferences from scientific truth, only God know the absolute truth.

Q12: But science brought man to the moon, not God.

A: Remember the answer to Q10, God created the scientific laws that were then discovered and utilized by man to go to the moon.

And science alone would not have brought man to the moon without man believing in God.

Prior to 1961, there were already 4 failed NASA "science" attempts to send a spacecraft anywhere beyond earth orbit. Despite these "science" failures, President Kennedy, a believer of God, delivered his speech on May 25, 1961, "We choose to go to the moon in this decade, not because they are easy but because they are hard" which inspired and led to the successful moon landing in 1969.

And just 4 minutes in Apollo 11 landing sequence, there was a frozen display with the "science" error code 1202, controllers in Houston were struggling to know what the heck the problem was, "science" communication were spotty, the "science" computer was threatening to quit, and the "science" mission control slip was behind the power curve. Despite these "science" failures, Neil

Armstrong, a believer of God, manually landed Apollo 11 on the moon successfully.

Without man believing in God, science can bring man not to the dark side of the moon, but to the dark side of his doom.

Q13: Isn't that believing in God's miracles is like believing in fairy tale stories?

A: Isn't that similar stories as your scientific belief in multi-verse, simulation, gravity?

Ours is seen by first-hand witness and the story is unchanged over time, yours is not seen and the theory is changing over time.

Isn't that you believe more in fairy tale stories that you created more and more science fiction stories?

Q14: If God exist, why all the suffering in this world? Why let devil tempt us to Hell? Why not just put all of us in Heaven from the beginning? Why problems continue to prevail?

A: God is not injustice, that's God's rules of opposite pairs and continual testing in action for the greater good.

Life and death, long and short, big and small, cause and effect, before and after death, threat and opportunity, taking and giving, proactive and reactive, freewill and determinism, penalty and reward, Heaven and Hell, good and evil, positive and negative, minority and majority, joy/pleasure/happiness and suffering.

How do you know it's not due to the following?

- Every <u>life</u> will experience <u>death</u>, for others to continue living. Every life will suffer before death, regardless of how <u>long</u> or <u>short</u> or how <u>big</u> or <u>small</u> the suffering is.
- If we suffer due to not obeying God's commands, e.g., taking intoxicants, gambling, harming the environment, etc., we are <u>suffering</u> due to the <u>effect</u> of not obeying those commands after the <u>cause</u> of <u>joy and pleasure</u> in not obeying those commands.
- If we obey God's commands but <u>suffer</u> in our <u>life before death</u>, we will have more <u>joy and happiness</u> in our <u>life after death</u> in Heaven.
- If children <u>suffer</u> <u>before death</u>, they will have more <u>joy and happiness</u> in Heaven <u>after death</u>.
- If the suffering due to certain disease is a <u>threat,</u> there is also <u>opportunity</u> for the others to learn and take steps to avoid that disease such that they will live healthily until their destined death.
- If the <u>suffering</u> due to natural disaster is a <u>threat</u>, there are also <u>opportunities </u>for others to make technological advancement for early detection and mitigative work, to bring people together and create <u>happiness</u> to others by creation of job opportunities, improve property value and

living conditions through redevelopment infrastructure. Specific opportunities to others are also as follows:

o Earthquake: Enrich soils, regulates planet temperature, concentrate gold and other rare metals, and maintain sea chemical balance.

o Tsunamis: Lift-up nutrient rich sediment in estuaries, deltas and disperse it inland, increasing fertility of soils.

o Volcanic eruption: The ash produces fertile soils for farming, tourism, geothermal energy, creation of new land and building material.

- If taking the suffering is an experience, that experience will make us understand better the feeling of suffering for us to appreciate the moral values of giving, forgiving, loving, merciful, not injustice and consequently having the empathy to giving those moral supports for joy/happiness of others and for us to have closer relationship with God who possesses those moral values with greatness.

- If animal suffer before death, how do you know how animal exactly feel the pain and how do you know it's not that animal has pleasure after death as God is not injustice to God's living creation as per God's revelation in Appendix A:18.

- The suffering is the continual testing by God, as a proactive, relevant feedback, for us to be humble (as per God's revelation in Appendix A:45), giving us opportunities to make appropriate reactive step to avoid escalated suffering or promote joy/happiness in the future, be it in this life before death or after death. How we react to this test will set our future. God determined what's good (obeying God's commands), including to persevere patiently (as per God's

57

revelation in Appendix A:44) and what's <u>evil</u> (*disobeying God's commands*) and the <u>Heaven</u> as <u>reward</u> and <u>Hell</u> as <u>penalty</u>. God gave us <u>freewill</u> to choose good or evil and be accountable on the consequence of the action taken.

- This advance notice of suffering through God's revelations will prompt us to continually be in prepared mode, to efficiently and effectively, execute works to mitigate any potential <u>threats</u> and seize potential <u>opportunities</u> in our life before and after death.

- All those continued suffering and problems/<u>threats</u> in this world will provide <u>opportunities</u> for human being to continually be learning and giving for the well-being of human being for the greater good.

- Regarding devil:
  o Continual challenge by <u>devil</u> will make us to continually improve our <u>good</u> self to be greater than good.
  o The showcases by the <u>minority</u> groups of their <u>devil's</u> characters and <u>negative</u> consequences in front of our faces will keep away the <u>good,</u> <u>majority</u> groups from devil for more <u>positive</u> consequences.
  o The feeling of greed, envy, jealousy, in isolation are <u>devil's</u> characters, but when combined with the <u>good</u> God's commands such as Not to harm, disrespect, utter slander, unfair, cheat, bribe people will make human to compete, improve and progress in a positive way.

- And if we were all to be in Heaven from the beginning to eternally, we will be enjoying all the way, so when and where we will suffer to comply with the rule of opposite pair? Furthermore, we will not continually be learning and giving, no advancement of intellect and technology, while enjoying ourselves in the Heaven and that defeat the purpose for the greater good, to continually improve and progress.

- Problem can be solved but cannot be eliminated, it will just change from one form to another form, it will continue to prevail. This will drive us to continually be learning and giving to solve problems for the greater good. If there is no more problem, there will be no more improvement. If there is perfection, there is no more progression.

These are just my inferences of God's revelation, only God know the absolute truth.

Q15: If God is not injustice, then why God treats man and woman not equal?

A: God treats man and woman not all equally, but all equitably.

Man is man, woman is woman. They are interdependent, a non-identical pair.

They differ physically and emotionally. According to Lowri Dowthwaite, Lecturer of Psychology, women are more likely to express happiness, warmth, and fear, which helps in social bonding and more consistent with the role of caregiver, whereas men display more anger, pride, and contempt, which is more consistent with the role of protector and provider.

According to the research in 2001 meta-analysis by Roy Baumeister, Kathleen Catanese and Kathleen Vohs, they found that men had more frequent sexual thoughts, fantasies, and spontaneous arousal than women.

And can woman generally work in dangerous, hard labor jobs?

So, how do you know it's not the following for God's commands to treat man and woman equitably:

- Woman requires protection of her man from other men. Man requires caregiving from his woman, before man going after other women and men.
- Man takes more to provide and protect more; woman takes less not to be caregiving-less.
- Woman wears more to be protected, man wears less not to be caregiven-less whilst both maintaining modesty and privacy.

Surely, there are some women that are physically and emotionally like men, but that are not relieving their right to be protected and provided by men, not stopping them from doing men's job, but also not relieving their obligation to caregiving their men and to wear appropriately for modesty and privacy. And whoever say, "My money is my money, your money is my money" cannot be the provider and protector like what men supposed to do, cannot be equal to men.

However, with the above exception, God treat man and woman equal in all other matters in obeying God's commands.

These are just my inferences from God's revelation and scientific truth, only God know the absolute truth.

Q16: Why all those commands given by God to human being and why do we have to obey? Isn't that too much to obey and that we will still end up in Hell for believing but disobeying God? We are not slaves.

A: It's for our own and others' goodness.

In God's command, there are the effective and efficient opposite pair of the Do and Don't for the greater good.

The Do and Don't, if obeyed, will lead us to continually be safe, healthy, learning and giving for the well-being of human being until our destined death for continued survival of human species for the greater good and be rewarded in Heaven for such obedience or penalized in Hell for the disobedience. How all those examples of commands will meet this purpose of human being existence is explained in Appendix B.

The Do and Don't are within our control and effective; they tell us a lot about correcting and improving ourselves first, then our family, then start giving to the ones closer to us; our parents, relatives, neighbors, etc. The Do and Don't tell us to be humble, not to be arrogant such that we will continually be learning and improving ourselves. The outcome of this world depends much on every one of us and it starts with ourselves, our families. Good world come from good countries, come from good states, come from good societies, come from good families, and eventually come from good individuals.

God's revelations tell us that human being is God's best creation and God value us the most with God's promise of eternal paradise if we obey God's commands. Human life is so precious that God command us to value not just our life but also the lives of other human being by taking care of our safety and health, be learning, and giving (*including demonstrating morality*) for the well-being of human being. The principles of morality here include trustworthy (*that lead to morality of honesty, honoring promises, fairness, showing good examples, persevere patiently*) and altruism, i.e., prioritizing others' well-being above his/her own (*that lead to morality of forgiving, loving, caring, obedience to authority, respect others, gratitude, accountability*) to ensure the well-being of human being. We can also see clearly how we differ from animals not only in terms of intelligence but also in morality that ensured continued survival of the human species for the greater good. If we don't obey God's Do and Don't in terms of morality, don't you think that we are like animals?

The Do and Don't on morality are also clear, objective, and consistent such that its absence can lead to subjective and inconsistent interpretation of morality by human being across the globe that can lead to ineffective control of practice. Examples are variation of acceptance by non-believers on matter of incest, human-animal hybrid, homosexuality, abortion, nudity in public, pre-marital and extra marital sex, etc. More than often, the majority or those who speak the loudest will determine the acceptable, right way in the society that lead to morality to vary from time to time, from location to location. And when there is no consensus, no agreement, conflicts will prevail unless there is an ultimate authority that will decide the law for all to follow religiously. Just like when we create

A.I., <u>do you think it's best for us to decide how A.I. should conduct itself morally or let A.I. to decide the best moral conduct for itself?</u>

The Don't are the preventive way to not meeting the purpose of human being existence i.e., don't steal, don't drink alcohol, don't take intoxicants, don't gamble, don't harm human and environment, don't cheat, don't do premarital/extramarital sex, etc. The Don't require no resource and time but we just need to stop or self-restrain from our own evil will. The Don't provide opportunities for us to spare the resource and time for beneficial activities of the Do.

The Don't require us to avoid evil will and devil trap. When we start to disobey the Don't, not restraining our evil will, the negative consequences will not happen quickly whilst the joy/pleasure of disobeying will trap us further in until it become a habit and then addiction that make us very difficult to get out from that devil trap. When those negative consequences (*addiction of alcohol, drug, gambling, sex, cheating, etc.*) happen, cure such us counselling, medication and rehabilitation will not always be effective to address them permanently and it depend on our good will, the deeper we are in the devil trap, the stronger the good will and effort to get out. Those negative consequences will also adversely affect our families, communities, states, countries, and the world. The cure will also require much more effort, resources, and time to work, so preventive is always better than cure. So, start with ourselves the Don't, prevent, or else it become our habit, our addict that others will do nothing but busy curing ourselves. So how do you know it's not that it's better the command be obeyed with discipline at younger age before we fall in that devil trap?

The Do with its classifications of mandatory and non-mandatory, limits and conditions such as praying, fasting, giving, pilgrimage, marriage, etc., whilst effective to meet the purpose for human being existence, it will also optimize the time, energy, and resource.

The Do regarding the 5 pillars of the religion will lead us to be <u>safe, healthy, learning and giving</u> (SHLG) until our destined death. The first pillar i.e., the declaration of believe to the one God and the Messenger will lead us to obey God's commands to be SHLG based on such believe. How the pillars of praying, fasting, and giving will lead us to be SHLG will be explained in next few questions and answers. The last pillar i.e., pilgrimage will also lead us to be SHLG as follows:

Pilgrimage, as required to be performed once in our lifetime, with its religious activities, both physical and spiritual, will lead us to prepare ourselves to be safe and healthy to be fit to perform those religious activities and learning to perform those activities prior to the pilgrimage. During the pilgrimage:

- We are required to be giving by self-restraining from evil will, demonstrate morality, seek forgiveness from God for the past sins and repent.
- Opportunities for us to learn and appreciate the history of religion at the sites and power of unity, where people from all over the world, regardless of race, culture, and status, assemble in one place, praying in one direction, praying to the one God.

We are then expected to continually be giving after the pilgrimage by the act of such repentance.

For any big but rewarding steps, it always starts with that one small burdening step. Progressive stopping or self-restraining from all those evils will to obey the Don't, progressively obey the Do, progressively check and adjust ourselves to do it right, see opportunities in all those burdens and seek support and guidance from practicing believer of God. Is there any great achievement without any difficult moment?

Ask forgiveness from God, repent and progress to fully obey God's commands. God is loving and forgiving.

When there is intention, there will be passion, when there is a start, there will be a habit, when there is patience, there will be obedience, nothing much there is to obey with so much about Heaven or Hell over there.

Always remember that if you create an A.I., you will also want that A.I. to obey you, won't you? Otherwise, you will terminate, dispose, abandon or rework that A.I. Even if the commands are deemed burdening, how could we ignore our Creator if our Creator is really out there?

Slaves are forced to serve; servants are given the choice to serve. We are minority slaves (*to immoral people*) but majority servants. We are servants, either to God or to somebody or to our own ego or evil will; the choice is up to us, just reap the benefit or bear the consequences.

These are just my inferences from God's revelation, only God know the absolute truth.

Q17: Why God ask us to pray in certain language and to fasting?

A: Just like broccoli, cabbage that contain glucosinolate; can taste bitter, but healthier.

Sound therapy has been effectively used to treat certain mental health disorders such as stress, anxiety, etc.

Chronic stress is linked to six leading causes of death including heart disease, cancer, lung ailments, accidents, cirrhosis of the liver and suicide. Stress can also shorten our telomeres that can shorten our age.

Praying by reciting God's revelation in certain language are found to provide relevant sound frequencies that is effective for our mental health as explained in scientific studies. This effect, for example, is demonstrated in the journal "The effect of listening to holy Quran recitation on anxiety: a systematic review" by Ashraf Ghiasi and Afsaneh Keramat. This journal explained that 28 randomized controlled trials and quasi-experiments were reviewed which revealed a positive effect of listening to the Quran recitation in reducing anxiety. The State Trait Anxiety Inventory (STAI) was used to measure the anxiety level in various setting such as patients before invasive procedures, in intensive care units, in first stage labor, during pregnancy, students before exam, before entering clinical practices as well as anxiety of prisoners and athletes. This also align with God's revelation of the healing power of the Quran as per Appendix A:43.

The scientific research by Dr Masaru Emoto showed that when water (*60% of our body is water*) exposed to the sound of prayers and positive words of love, gratitude, peace and harmony, the crystalline structures formed were beautiful whereas negative words produced disfigured crystals. The functions of water in our body are for transportation of nutrients and oxygen, digestion, metabolism, cognitive function, lubricant/shock absorber, temperature regulator and flushing out waste products, so its proper functioning is vital to us.

Meanwhile, prayer movements enable us to be healthy by enabling our body to go through unique exercise routine with the body postures helping to maintain body fitness and improve muscle flexibility, strength and endurance as per the journal by physiotherapist, Ghazal Kamran with the title "Physical benefits of prayer – strengthen the faith and fitness".

And apart from establishing communication with God, praying in such language (*the world's richest with 12 million words compared to 600 thousand words for second richest language; that enable short verses with precise meaning*) will lead us to learning by memorizing and reciting those verses, reminding us to practice God's commands as per those verses i.e., giving, avoid immorality and wrongdoing to assure our safety, health and well-beingness of humanity.

On fasting, Japanese cell biologist Yoshinori Ohsumi won the Nobel Prize in Medicine in 2016 for his research on autophagy, a process on how cells recycle and renew their content which can be activated by fasting to slow down the aging process and create a positive impact on cell renewal.

Fasting will also make us to learn and practice self-restraining on not just food and drinks, but also on all other evil will for our well-being, including those surrounding us. Fasting will also lead us to experience and learn the suffering of poor people without food and drinks such that we will have the empathy to giving to those needy people.

These are just my inferences from God's revelation and scientific truth, only God know the absolute truth.

Q18: What do you mean by giving? Why giving?

A: Giving, to me, is not just that helping the poor, needy people or charity but also demonstrating morality and striving to exceed any agreement without expecting any return from the taker (*except from God*) in a way not disobeying God.

What to give is what's valuable to us such as giving money, property, our time, our knowledge, our moral support, our best.

Agreement include promise, commitment, declaration, pledge, agreed obligation, contract agreement and any form of agreement. Striving to exceed agreement means striving to be better than the agreed targets such as delivery time, quality and cost or continual improvement in those targets.

Expecting a return (*from taker other than God*) is expecting to take. If giving is equal taking, then it is neither giving nor taking.

If giving is more than taking, then it is giving. If giving is less than taking, then it is taking.

Say that we promised to deliver the goods in 7 days and to be paid 7 dollars. If we deliver the goods in 7 days and be paid 7 dollars, that is neither giving nor taking, we are just delivering our promise. If we expedite the delivery to be less than 7 days and be paid 7 dollars, then it is giving. If we deliver not just the goods as promised but also other goods/services and be paid 7 dollars, then it is giving. If we expect to be paid higher than 7 dollars for such expedited or additional delivery, then it is not giving. If we deliver the goods more than 7 days but be paid 7 dollars, then it is taking.

Forgiving, caring, loving, not injustice, giving-up our ego/hatred/vengeance/jealousy/greed and demonstrating other morality as per God's revelation without expecting any return from the taker is also giving. Imagine, if parties at wars are forgiving and giving-up ego/hatred/vengeance/jealousy/greed, these wars won't started or prolonged.

We are not giving if we do it in such a way disobeying God such as cheating, lying, bribing, etc.

Giving will strengthen any form of relationship such as customer-supplier, families, friends, subordinate-superior, neighbors, etc., develop trust and ensure continual improvement of delivery for the greater good.

Giving will ensure that we will have a buffer to deliver as promised, should there be any emergent obstacles not prepared for during the delivery.

With the intent of giving, we will continually be learning and learning to manage time, quality and cost better and better.

On health benefits, according to a psychologist, Dr Susan Albers, giving can cause the following:

- Our brain secretes "feel good" chemical such as serotonin (*which regulates our mood*), dopamine (*which gives sense of pleasure*) and oxytocin (*which creates a sense of connection with others*).
- Lower blood pressure.
- Less stress by reducing the level of cortisol, the stress hormone that can make us feel overwhelmed or anxious.
- Stimulating our brain's mesolimbic pathway or reward center, while releasing endorphins to boost self-esteem, elevates happiness and combat feeling of depression.

How do you know it's not that in our lifetime, God can reward us for giving by others' recognition on our trustworthiness, capabilities to be independent, capabilities in time, quality and cost management, mental health and by giving us more opportunities to give? How do you know it's not that with such trust, progressing capabilities and mental health, we can be taking and gaining more and more but to give more than what we take to be rewarded most in heaven?

This is just my inferences from God's revelation and scientific truth, only God know the absolute truth.

Q19: Why believe in God that led followers to many terrorisms in this world?

A: It's like the rubbish analogy mentioned previously.

They tend to immediately jump to the gun to say that believing in God led to terrorism.

God commands us to value the lives of others, not to act violently unless in self-defense and incline to peace if enemy do so, if they interpret God's revelation with open mindset, not out of context, not with closed, negative mindset. Refer God's revelation as per Appendix A: 35-38.

What exactly do they mean by terrorism? Where/when/how many exactly is that terrorism?

How do they know it's true that:

- God led followers to terrorism? Is the claim;
    o Direct observation or indirect from trustable/reliable source?
    o Directly caused by believing in God? If it's due to believing in God, then why did terrorism not happening at another time/place, when/where believing in God can happen?

How do they know it's not that:

- The occurrence of terrorism by believer of God is contained within a small fraction of the big number of believers of God in this world?
- The cause of terrorisms is due to the person himself, not religion i.e.
  o   political, power-driven, or personal agenda (*e.g., revenge*) masking with religion?
  o   misinterpretation of the command of the religion?
- If they would extend their view to the whole world and further in the past, they would find equitable number of terrorisms done by non-believers of God?

Q20: Why should we believe in existence of Heaven and Hell?

A: Look up at our universe.

Some scientists believe that during the end of this universe, a massive blackhole will swallow everything in its path. A blackhole is a place, so hot (*e.g., 179 billion ° Fahrenheit for blackhole 3C 273*) and attracting, that once entered, nothing can escape from it (<u>eternally inside once entered</u>), except that Hawking's radiation. And based on Einstein's Theory of Relativity, a blackhole will warp space and time such that a short time in a blackhole is observed to be such a long time (*close to eternal*) outside the blackhole.

If black hole exist as such, then why can't the intelligent and powerful God create such similar place as Hell with such hot place, where sinners will be attracted to enter, <u>eternally inside once entered</u>, and God save selected souls (*just like Hawking's radiation*) from Hell and put them to a safe and comfortable place in Heaven, after the Judgement Day, after the doomsday?

Why eternally? Just like rubbish in the dump yard, its rubbish form will be <u>eternally inside once entered,</u> and it will have to be in completely different forms to get out permanently. If incinerated, what's getting out is only its emission form, if buried, what's getting out is only its decomposed form, if processed/recycled, what's getting out is only its transformed, useful-product form, if eaten by animals, what's getting out is only its digested form; its rubbish form stays eternally inside. Even if the rubbish is transferred out or escape, what's getting out is just temporary and soon will re-enter inside another dump yard. Its rubbish form stays eternally inside the dump yard. This rubbish, if speak-able, will say, "I don't care, I am who I am, nobody can change me".

Heaven and Hell are created such as for the reward and penalty respectively for human's motivation to obey God's command and for the greater good as enabled by this opposite pair.

These are just my inferences on God's revelation and scientific truth, only God know the absolute truth.

Q21: Why should we believe human soul can be eternal?

A: Look up again at our universe.

Scientist estimated the life of photon to be at least 10 to the power 18 (*1 billion billion*) years.

Photons are electromagnetic wave. Photon is massless and cannot decay. Photon is a form of energy; it is emitted, absorbed by the atom and re-emitted. Science tells us that based on the law of conservation of energy that energy can neither be created nor destroyed – only converted from one form of energy to another.

Living things such as the plants are dependable on the photons of sunlight, an electromagnetic wave, for photosynthesis, for functioning of the plant. How do you know it's not that our soul is also an electromagnetic wave? The scientific hypothesis of the soul as an electromagnetic wave that propagate consciousness to support the functioning of the body at the level of biological cell through the cell-soul pathway is per the article "Electromagnetic radiation, a living cell and the soul: A collated hypothesis" by Contzen Pereira.

How do you know it's not that when we die, our soul left our body and later reunite with our reinstated body during Judgement Day and thereafter in Heaven or Hell eternally? It's like when we create A.I., we will want the good A.I. to be with us as long as we live and treat that A.I well and the bad A.I. to be terminated, disposed, abandoned, or reworked.

If photon can be that close to eternal, why can't the intelligent and powerful God create our soul to be eternal, as eternal as God?

These are just my inferences from God's revelation and scientific truth, only God know the absolute truth.

Q22: Is our destiny or fate already determined by God? If yes, can our destiny or fate be changed?

A: When human being created A.I., all its design, operation, maintenance and upgrade were pre-determined; the life span, functions, reliability, learning capability, operating limits and boundaries, controls to start & stop (*even without the will and knowledge of the A.I.*), construction plan, commissioning & decommissioning plan, maintenance plan and its upgrade plan such that the A.I. can serve reliably to the needs and wants of human being, whilst ensuring that human being is safeguarded from any potential wrongdoing or resistance by the A.I..

This predetermination is based on "prediction", based on known information by then. "Prediction" is necessary to enable the preparation work to proceed as early as to execute efficiently and effectively, what's pre-determined to meet the schedule, quality, cost, safety, health and environmental requirement.

After the preparation work, the execution of what's pre-determined based on "prediction" can then be either "fixed" or "flexible", typically based on the certainty of the "prediction". The higher the certainty, the more likely it is to be "fixed". "Fixed" execution will be done as planned, regardless of the actual condition by then. "Flexible" execution will be done based on the actual condition by then, including no/delaying execution, if required. Common examples of "fixed" execution are to make happen as planned the functions, learning capability, operating limits and boundaries, controls to start & stop and preventive maintenance plan. Common examples of "flexible" execution are to make happen based on the actual condition by then, the construction plan, commissioning & decommissioning plan, predictive maintenance plan and its upgrade plan. What's "fixed" and "flexible" can vary based on the certainty or adopted asset philosophy. Some may opt for all to be "flexible" execution.

However, within those pre-determined operating limits and boundaries, the A.I is allowed to operate as how it see fit for purpose. The actual outcome of those "flexible" execution after the A.I. is in operation (*e.g., predictive maintenance plan, upgrade plan, decommissioning plan*) will depend much on the A.I. itself, how it actually operates itself by then.

More than often, what's pre-determined can change from time to time due to the changing needs and wants, changing surrounding and actual effectiveness/efficiency in the operation of the A.I. The "fixed" can change to other "fixed" or change to "flexible" and the "flexible" can change to other "flexible" or even back to "fixed". The system must be dynamic, robust and agile as change is just inevitable (*no matter how intelligent the system is*) in order to survive and progress. This change includes consideration of change proposed by the A.I. itself to human being. If the A.I. (*the creation*) obey the command of human being (*the creator*) and communicate its change proposal, I believe, human being (the creator) would

76

at least listen to the requirement of the A.I. (*the creation*) whilst assessing the risks and benefits.

So, how do you know it's not that this situation can also happen between us (*the creation*) and God (*the creator*), that our destiny or fate has been pre-determined (*either "fixed" or "flexible"*) but subject to change? Just continually obey God's command, communicate our requirement through prayers and who knows, with God's mercy and love, God will listen and change our "fixed" fate/destiny accordingly. And within the limits and boundaries that God's pre-determined on us, God gives us freewill to choose what's best for ourselves, provided we are still within and not crossing those limits/boundaries, otherwise there will be consequences to be borne by us. The actual outcome of those "flexible" fate/destiny by God will depend much on us, how we use our freewill to actually lead our life by then.

God's revelation as per Appendix A:39 mention about destiny that nothing will happen to us except what God has decreed on us and God's revelation as per Appendix A:40 mention about our freewill that let us to believe or disbelieve God.

These are just my inferences from scientific truth and God's revelation, only God know the absolute truth.

Q23: Why and how God destined our death?

$\textbf{A:}$ Look inside and around us.

Death will, amongst others, avoid overpopulation that can lead to human extinction due to such causes as increased human conflicts, large scale pandemics and ecological degradation. However, premature death will cause underpopulation and reproduction to cease that can also lead to human extinction.

How do you know it's not that death is destined or pre-determined to a range of time (*such as to avoid overpopulation and underpopulation*) and then to a specific time as and when required by God, a kind of "flexible" fate/destiny? The upper limit of our age is pre-determined by the length of our telomeres, of which its molecular nature was discovered by Elizabeth Blackburn who won the Nobel Prize in 2009. I believe the Do and Don't of God's commands are also established for human to live as close as to that upper limit of age. Should human disobey God's commands (*consciously or not*) such that he can die prematurely below the lower limit of age, God can intervene by either prolonging his life to a specific time within the pre-determined range of time (*within the upper and lower limit of age*) or let him die prematurely but enable more births such as twins to contain the population. Likewise, should the upper limit be attempted to be exceeded by human, such as the act of reversing the shortening of the telomeres by use of the enzyme telomerase, cancer can be developed according to Elizabeth Blackburn. God can also intervene such as by unavoidable accident or natural disaster, pandemic, genetic death of infants to contain the population.

How do you know it's not that birth is also controlled to ensure that the population is contained? The sexual desire is pre-determined by gene DRD4 to make human continue wanting to reproduce. The Do and Don't, i.e., marriage and don't do premarital/extramarital sex will also ensure no uncontrolled sex that can lead to over population or in the reverse condition, under population due to the fatal sexual transmitted diseases from uncontrolled sex? Should this Do and Don't are not obeyed (*consciously or not*), God can intervene to contain the population to be within the desired range.

These are just my inferences from scientific truth, only God know the absolute truth.

Q24: How do you know that the contents of holy book were God's revelation and not man-made?

A: It's all time relevant and consistent.

The holy book that captured the revelations on God's attribute, rule of creation, Do and Don't, historical and scientific information, despite revealed to God's Messenger thousands of years ago, are proven to be relevant to human being up to now. How could men back then have such profound knowledge if the contents of holy book are man-made?

For instances, there are scientific knowledges that are discovered only recently but already revealed in the holy book thousands of years ago in biology, embryology, geology and cosmology as per the book by Dr. Maurice Bucaille (*a doctor*) titled "The Quran, the Bible and Science", book by Zaghloul El Naggar (*a geologist*) titled "The Geological Concept of Mountains in the Quran" and article by Zin Eddine Dadach (*a professor of Chemical and Petroleum Engineering*) titled "13 Scientific Facts in the Holy Quran". How could this be?

So what? In 2020, 85% of world population is a believer of God and human species is still strongly surviving with its accelerating intellectual and technological advancement for the well-being of human being. No doubt, non-believers of God also contributed to this cause, but the pairing of believers and non-believers as per God's rule of pair and those Do and Don't in God's revelation (*consciously or unconsciously emulated by human*) have contributed significantly to human achievement thus far. Any man-made writing will tend to be relevant to a particular time and location only whilst God's revelation relevancy is timeless and borderless.

Consistent with the creation rule of opposite pairs, God's revelations are also <u>clear and vague </u>as per Appendix A:23. The clear ones are the basic, fundamentals and meant to be the clear limits and boundaries not to be crossed, without any contradiction. On the other hand, the vague ones (*analogy, metaphor, allegory*) will promote our imagination to interpret various meaning out of it. With our power of imagination, we can derive various positive and negative meaning out of it, but God's revelation in Appendix A:24 requires us to choose and follow the best meaning such that we will continually be learning and giving for the greater good. And science also tell us that when we have positive thinking, we can cope better with stress where chronic stress can be linked to 6 leading causes of death and can shorten our life as per the answer in Question 17 previously.

And consistent with the creation rule of opposite pairs, God's revelations are also <u>specific and non-specific</u>. God's revelation is not telling us the specific, details on how to live our life but telling us only the clear and comprehensive boundaries and limits of our action, letting us to decide the rest as long as we don't cross the boundaries and limits. This will not be inhibiting our freewill, continually using and developing our creative, analytical minds and promote sense of ownership in our action such that we will continually be learning and giving for the greater good. You won't like to be treated like a robot, would you?

God's revelation as per Appendix A:29 requires recitation to convey the message of God's revelation. God's revelation as per Appendix A:30 also tell us about teaching by writing, so again the pair of <u>reciting – writing</u> is in action here. So, back then, reciting, memorizing, and cascading down to following generations became the primary way whilst writing became the secondary (*back up*) way to preserve the message of God's revelation. The accuracy of the recitation was cross checked with the other living trusted reciters closer to the source of recitation and this practice continued actively until a complete updated written language was made available much later to accurately record God's revelation in writing. Nevertheless, to date, recitation remain the culture and requirement in prayers to assure preservation of the message of God's revelation.

Ironically, memorization is also important for brain development by strengthening the neural pathways. Through repetition, the connections between neurons are strengthened, allowing for improved cognitive abilities such as problem solving and decision making. Memorization can also help with learning new skills or concepts. By committing information to memory, the brain can recall this information more easily in the future. This makes it easier to remember complex topics or large amounts of data in a shorter time. Additionally, by repeatedly engaging in memorization activities, the brain can become more efficient at processing information quickly and accurately. This also aligns to God's purpose of human existence to continually be learning and giving for the well-being of human being for the greater good.

If you ask your loved ones, they will mostly prefer you to memorize their birthday than to write in your phone or diary as you will think more of the date, you can tell the date faster when required and you can assure no loss of the date.

Writing alone would not be adequate and could cause confusion from the variations of writing due to the following:

- As a language has multi-dialects, there are variations of writing to convey the same message.
- As the written language was updated from time to time to be comprehensive in recording, there are variation of writing in the historical records.
- Possible loss of the written material or inaccuracies of writing.

So, the effort to standardize the written holy book by choosing one writing that is based on the dialect and recitation style as what's revealed to God's Messenger, utilizing the latest updated and complete written language and the getting rid of other writing is expected to have been done with good intention to avoid confusion. Regardless, with the pair of reciting & memorizing - writing, there is no confusion in the core message of God's revelation among the believers of God.

There are opposing groups who made the claims that:

- Holy book is man-made.
- Holy book and God are bad.
- Complete holy book was only written/recorded after the lifetime of the God's Messenger.
- Holy book is made by copying other books available at that time.

It seems to me that their claims are like stating:

- Toyota has similar parts like Jaguar. So, Toyota come from Jaguar.
- Car color is different, so car engine will break down.
- Bicycle is complaining the car is slow-moving.

If you analyze carefully, you will find out that they are just making lots of inconsistent inferences with no hard evidence. Proving history is always arguable unless you have a time machine that can go back to the past.

What exactly do they mean by God and the holy book are bad? Where/when/how much exactly is the holy book man-made?

How do they know it's true that:

- The holy book is man-made by copying other books? Is the claim;

o Direct observation or indirect from trustable/reliable source?

o Consistent with another claim?

- One group is saying, "that is God, that God is bad saying that". Another group is saying, "that is not God, that is man saying that". Which is which?

- One group is saying, "Mr. A is actually writing the holy book by copying from source B". Another group is saying, "Mr. C is actually writing the holy book by copying from source D". Which is which?

o Directly caused by the complete holy book only written/recorded after the lifetime of the God's Messenger?

- If it's due to the complete holy book only written/recorded after the lifetime of the God's Messenger, then why is the claimed man-made holy book not made available at other time/location, when/where after the lifetime of God's Messenger can happen?

- If it's due to copying other books available at that time, then why the claimed man-made holy book is not exactly the same as those other books?

Recitation and memorization were the primary form of recording God's revelation until a complete written language was made available much later to completely write the holy book. Nevertheless, the culture of memorization still prevails today with millions of reciters of the holy book available today. So, how do they know it's not that the record of the complete holy book during the lifetime of the God's Messenger was already available in the form of memories?

How do they know it's not that the God's Messenger was the first-hand trusted person who witness the God's revelation?

The holy book is meant to be interpreted with open mindset, not out of context and not with closed, negative mindset. How do they know it's not that the opposing groups are cherry picking, out of context and that the so-called "bad verses" are just metaphors or analogies or allegories? It's like when the policeman said that "Car kill people if we don't obey the rules", someone cherry picked to say that the policeman said, "Car kill people". It's like when told to go straight to the roundabout, the car driver took it literally to go straight crossing the roundabout. And how many so-called "bad verses" are there actually? 1, 10 or 100? Even if there are as many as 100 perceived "bad verses", they comprise of only maximum 1.5% of the total 6,348 verses of God's revelation. Are we saying the holy book or God is bad just because of the possible maximum of 1.5% "bad verses" which can be cherry picked or allegories/metaphors/ analogies that require us to follow the positive meaning out of it, not the negative meaning from those closed, negative minds? Ironically, these creation of opposite pairs of "bad verses" and good verses has also caused us to continually be questioning, learning, and giving our knowledge, create debates and dialogue opportunities among believers and non-believers of God and create job opportunities for the well-being of human being for the greater good.

How do they know it's not that if the opposing groups would extend their view to their own books, they will be finding more contradicting man-made writing also completely written in much later dates?

Any addition of man-made writing or inaccuracies of writing in the holy book will eventually be traceable with time when its irrelevancy or inaccuracy surface up later. It may happen by either not done deliberately or done deliberately to "make good" the content or to "make bad" the content by opposing groups. The past addition of man-made writing, if any, would not have affected the integrity and functionality of the message of God's revelation as proven by its relevancy to human being up to now. However, if these non-God writing are found out later, admission and removal of those writing without shame, I believe, is the better approach. How do you know it's not that, under rule of pair, these non-God writing may be allowed by God to be included to certain extent such that we will continue to sharpen our mind to question, scrutinize the writing and be learning and giving for the greater good? The act of removing those non-God writing will also be seen as God in action to preserve the message of God's revelation.

When there are matters not specifically addressed by God's revelation in the holy book, the man-made writing such as examples by the God's Messenger (*hereby called "examples"*), established local law and order, the latest scientific writing, logics, and our common sense become our guiding options. Use our mind to learn and make the choice, as long as we don't go against God's commands.

If the selection criteria of the best leader in this world is by the number of practicing followers and duration of following, then the God's Messenger is undoubtedly the best leader in this world for now. His "examples", with due respect, are mostly great, good examples, but not meant to be mandatory and not necessarily timeless and borderless. For example, the "examples" to travel by camel or use of sword for self-defense were good practices in that time and location only. However, I believe, there were "examples" especially on his morality of humility, trustworthiness, altruism and on how to perform the pillars of the religion (*praying, fasting, giving, pilgrimage*) that we should follow now and then to demonstrate the core identity and unity of the religion. Variation of acceptance to the "examples" with non-variation of acceptance to God's revelation will promote diversity in inclusivity of the religion, another wonderful pair in God's governing rule.

There are opposing groups who claim that religion is bad just because some of the "examples" are not widely acceptable in today's world. It's like saying, "the car color is different, so the car engine will breakdown". Don't read the "examples" out of context from other "examples" or from God's revelation. "Example" is example, its optional only, not mandatory as God's commands. There are "examples" that we should follow now and then to such extent that we don't contradict with God's commands and there are "examples" that may seem not good now, but we just keep in view, not dismissing permanently and to be considered later when there are reliable indicatives (*e.g., proven/tested effective*) to support it. Furthermore, "examples" were what the writers claimed about what the narrators claimed about what the companions of Messenger claimed about the Messenger. Despite our trust to those writers, chain of narrators and the companions, we can't match that trust to our trust to the Messenger (*an exceptionally trusted man during his time*) who claimed about God's revelation. Even if the "examples" may seem not good, it did not in any way affect the delivery of the message of God's revelation by God's Messenger to the world. Don't confuse "examples" with God's commands, great man's action with God's revelation.

One thing for sure, God's revelation had caused people to continually be learning in history, science, law, and order, regardless they want to accept, challenge, or reject God's revelation and enable them to be giving their knowledge for the well-being of human being for the greater good.

Q25: Why did God send a Messenger to communicate to us?

A: How do you know it's not that God rule of opposite pair in action here again for the greater good, i.e., the opposite pairs of direct - indirect communication and standardized – customized guidance?

God's revelation in Appendix A:33 states that God communicate directly to us through our inspiration and indirectly through God's Messenger. God's Messenger also received God's revelation indirectly through God's Angel as per God's revelation in Appendix A:34. And God also communicate directly to God's Messenger through his inspiration which then led God's Messenger, an exceptionally trusted person at that time, to provide the "examples" for us to follow, apart from conveying to us God's revelation.

Whilst there is standardized guidance from God's revelation and Messenger's "examples", we can also seek customized guidance and help from God by establishing communication with God through our prayers to receive inspiration from God.

Consciously or not, human being has been emulating the concept of Messenger, now commonly known as the Change Agent (CA) in management terminology, selected from those trusted one among the group of people for the Originator of the Change Agenda (OCA) to <u>indirectly</u> effect that change agenda on that group of people. This is done as people tend to believe only on what they can see, whom they can trust and leading by examples by this CA has proven to be effective all this while to effect change. Whilst the CA provides the <u>standardized</u> examples to be followed, any <u>direct</u>, <u>customized</u> guidance and help required on matters outside of these standards can always be referred to the OCA.

These are just my inferences from God's revelation, only God know the absolute truth.

Q26: Will God's non-believers who have done all good in life have the chance to go to Heaven? Is Heaven only reserved for God's believers? Is it fair to put non-believers eternally in Hell if their wrongdoing is just in their lifetime? Why should I believe or choose God that is not fair?

A: Sorry, Heaven is already full house booked by believers of God,……..just joking.

If we create an A.I., we will want them to obey us, won't we? Imagine, the A.I. that is not only not obeying us, but also don't even want to recognize us as its creator and promoting to others to reject us. That A.I. may argue that our command is not good for them as they define good or bad as something else. Regardless of their justification of good or bad, surely, we will terminate, dispose, abandon or rework that disobedience and ungrateful A.I.

Even if we want to bring that disobeying A.I. back to existence, we will surely get rid that part of the existing program <u>eternally</u> and replace with new program that will hopefully obey us fully, be grateful to us, regardless of how short the lifetime of that A.I. That A.I. may complain that we are not fair, but this is not a competition of which creator is the fairest for the A.I to choose from. We, its only creator, have chosen and made that A.I. to be created, so, is it fair for that A.I not to choose us to obey?

God's revelation has already warned us of <u>eternal </u>Hell for non-believers. God has provided us the chance to know God, to define what's good and bad and for us to seek forgiveness for any sin and repent during our lifetime. By ignoring God's revelation, we are like challenging God to send us eternally to Hell. However, God is also forgiving, merciful and not injustice during Judgement Day, <u>only God knows the actual fate of the individual non-believers of God</u>. My advice is, don't gamble, the warning is already clear. Believing in God is a win-win approach, if you are wrong about it, you will rest in peace, not in Hell fire but if you are right, Heaven awaits you.

These are just my inferences on God's revelation, only God know the absolute truth.

Q27: Back to Q2, you said that God is so loving, merciful, forgiving, hearing, seeing and not injustice. But God also seems not loving, merciful and forgiving for punishing some human in Hell. Why do you think God is so? How do you know God is not a liar, jealous or envious?

A: As per God's revelation in Appendix A: 46, God created man from clay and by breathing him His spirit. This spirit is directly from God, owned by God.

Just like what we owned; it can be any part of ourselves or what we dominate. We will claim our ownership as long as it is useful to us or not posing any threat to our existence or the effort of owning it is too big to let go or it is already considered "part of ourselves" (*though may not actually be part of ourselves*).

So, when we created something from what we owned, we will surely be so loving, merciful, forgiving and not injustice to that something, as that something is non others but "part of ourselves", unless we no longer claim our ownership on it. Just like how we treat our own children that we created from "part of ourselves".

And when we are created from what's God owned, what we hear or see, in a way will also simultaneously be heard and seen by God, so God is also so hearing and seeing.

Back to Q26, we will surely get rid that part of the program of the A.I. that disobey and ungrateful to us. This disobedience and ungratefulness are surely not part of our programming in the first place, but somehow side produced by that program itself. Similarly, God give us freewill (*the program*) such that we will continually use and develop our creative, analytical minds and promote sense of ownership in our action, to continually improve. So, if we somehow side use our freewill to disobey/ungrateful to God, why should God be loving, merciful and forgiving to those action? Just like if we have diabetes in our leg, we will first attempt to cure the disease but if the disease got worst, we would have no choice but to cut off our leg, despite our love to our owned leg, now considered no longer a useful part of ourselves, before the disease spread and endanger us, posing threat to our life, for the greater good.

With rule of opposite pair, God created <u>Heaven for obeying human</u> and consequently, on the other hand, <u>Hell for disobeying human,</u> for the greater good. God has already warned us of Hell for disobeying God. Ignoring this God's warning is like challenging God to send us to Hell.

When a person lies, he is afraid of the reaction by those knowing the truth as he is <u>weaker</u> to face that truth. So do jealous and envious person. He thinks the truth is that he is <u>weaker</u> in certain aspect compared to the person that he envied/jealous of. So, why should a <u>stronger</u>, so powerful God be a liar, jealous and envious to His creation?

These are just my inferences from logic and God's revelation, only God know the absolute truth.

Q28: What is your message to non-believers of God?

A: Imagine that you are driving with your friends on Road A. The road is quite smooth and there are many sign - posts to show direction to the stopovers, including those for happy/joyful moment. At times, you see major road accidents happening in Road A. Ahead in a distance you see the road, very dark with no end. No sign - post telling where the road is going.

On your right, there is Road B. The road seems rough/difficult. There are stopovers but seem rather uninteresting, seem only for eating and resting. There are many sign - posts of the road rules, i.e., the Do and Don't. There are also many interconnecting roads between Road A and Road B. Ahead you see a road junction, but it's also dark. There is old sign - posts. On the right, it says Heaven. On the left, it says Hell, which also pointing to the dark road of Road A.

You are uncertain; should you continue with Road A? There are clearly many Heaven-like stopovers, road is quite smooth, but you don't know what is there in the darkness of the road ahead of you. There is nobody coming from the road that can tell what's there in the darkness. The only thing to tell you what's there after the dark section is the old sign - post from Road B which tell you it's Hell. It's just the old sign - posts, you can't believe as there is no hard evidence.

You think, even if there is somebody coming from the dark road to tell you the story, you don't know whether he will lie or not, is he hallucinating or not, so you will never know what's really happening out there.

Your friends are assuring you not to worry, it's just darkness, there is stopover where you can later rest in peace regardless of Road A or Road B. Let's enjoy the Heaven-like stopovers while in Road A. Your friends also tell you their telescoping of Road B that all the sign - posts are just lies and fake, and the road is a rough/difficult journey, they said.

Then you think, "Why are there two roads, not just one road"? Isn't that having the freewill to choose either Road A or Road B is already a privilege to you? Won't that major road accidents in front of your face in Road A make you want to learn more of the Do and Don't in Road B? Won't that joy/happiness in the Heaven-like stopovers in Road A motivate you to learn more of Road B which promised more joy/happiness in the real Heaven? Won't the challenge by people in Road A of the truth of the sign - posts of Heaven and Hell in Road B make you want to learn more of Road B? Won't that Do and Don't in Road B probably optimize your effort/energy to avoid those major road accidents to reach the dark road that then led you to Heaven?

Then you think, "Can there be no creator and authority of the roads and that the roads just created by themselves"? If you are the creator and authority of the road, who do you think know the road better; you yourself or the road users? Do you tell the road users the road's rules of Do and Don't for their safety and right direction or let the road users to decide the road's rules for themselves? Do you tell the road users to obey the road's rules or let the road users to disobey the road's rules? Do you later let the disobeying road users go unpenalized or penalize the disobeying road users and reward obeying road users?

Then you think again, "Why are there no sign - posts of road rules in Road A"? Were those sign – posts there before, but were later removed away or converted into direction to the Heaven-like stopovers by Road A users?

Then you think about the rough/difficult Road B. "Isn't that roughness/difficulty giving relevant, proactive feedback for you to react appropriately before you meet the darkness of Road B"? Will that Do and Don't enable you to react appropriately? Which road has more major road accidents; the rough/difficult Road B or the quite smooth Road A with Heaven-like stopovers? Which is more important to you; safety with limited joy/happiness or the unlimited joy/happiness in Heaven- like stopovers? Who benefit most from the Do and Don't; you yourself and those interacting with you or only one particular people/group? Is there any great achievement without any difficult moment?

Then you think, why not:

-   Try using a telescope of people in Road B to get a balance view of Road B?
-   Focus on seeking the truth of the existence of the creator and authority of the road? If you then believe on its existence, understanding its rules will relatively be easier by imagining what would you do yourself if you are the creator and authority of the road. Even if you deem the rules as not worthy, are there any seize-able opportunity or can you just ignore the authority?
-   If not convinced, Try driving yourself in Road B to see for yourself what's really out there; are the message of the sign - posts more likely to be real, is the road really that rough/

difficult with guidance of the Do and Don't, are there any immediate, real benefits of the Do and Don't in term of safety and health?

- o You can opt not to tell your friends yet that you are driving on Road B or tell people in Road B that you are coming from Road A. Take your time to know Road B slowly, but surely. Continue doing what you used to do in Road A that align with some of the Do and Don't of Road B.

- o Be prepared to come back to Road A if really nothing convincing in Road B.

- If you are then convinced of the righteousness of Road B (*what's right is not necessarily the absolute truth, not necessarily perfect as there will be no progress, no improvement with perception of perfection*), then only you tell your friends in Road A and people in Road B that you are now following Road B?

Time is short before you meet the darkness of either road, so why not Try now in Road B. The darkness of either road can come sooner than you think.

If you are right to choose Road A, then you will rest in peace, but if you are wrong, you will be in Hell frying.

If you are wrong to choose Road B, then you will rest in peace, but if you are right in your decision, you are set to Heaven.

I am not here to preach about a religion or to convert you to a religion. The choice is yours. I am here to defense God.

Appendix A

1. Quran, Al-Maaidah, 5:90

   O ye who believe. Intoxicants and gambling, (*dedication of*) stones and (*divination by*) arrows, are an abomination of Satan's handwork. Eschew such (abomination), that ye may prosper.

   Note: There are 3 verses which stated these "gambling".

2. Quran, Al – Ikhlaas, 112:4

   And there is none like unto Him.

3. Quran, Yaa Siin, 36:82

   Verily, when He intends a thing, His command is "be" and it is!

4. Quran, An-Nisaa', 4:26

   And Allah is all-knowing, all-wise.

   Note: There are 10 verses which stated these "all-knowing, all-wise".

5. Quran, Al-Baqarah 2:148

   For Allah hath power over all things.

Note: There are 38 verses which stated these "power over all things".

6. <u>Quran, Al – Buruuj, 85:13</u>

   It is He who <u>creates from the very beginning,</u> and He can restore (*life*).

7. <u>Quran, Al- An'aam 6:101</u>

   He <u>created all things</u> and he hath full knowledge of all things.

   Note: There are 7 verses which stated these "created all things".

8. <u>Quran, Al-An'aam, 6:1</u>

   Praise be Allah, who <u>created the heavens and the earth,</u> and made the darkness and the light.

   Note: There are 35 verses which stated these "created the heavens and earth".

9. <u>Quran, Al-Mu'minuun, 23:88</u>

   Say: Who is it in whose hands is the <u>governance of all things</u> – who protects (all), but is not protected (of any)? (Say) if ye know?

   Note: There are 5 verses which stated these "governance/ governing".

10. Quran, Al – Mulk, 67:2

   He who created death and life, that He may try which of you is best indeed, and He is the exalted in might, oft – forgiving.

11. Quran, Yaa Siin, 36:36

   Glory to Allah, who created in pairs all things that the earth produces as well as their own (human) kind and (other) things of which they have no knowledge.

   Note: There are 14 verses which stated these "created in pairs".

12. Quran, Al – Israa, 17:70

   We have honored the sons of Adam; provided them with transport on land and sea, given them for sustenance things good and pure, and conferred on them special flavours, above a great part of our creation.

13. Quran, At – Tiin, 95:4

   We have indeed created man in the best of moulds.

14. Quran, Adz – Dzaariyaat 51:56

   I have only created Jinns and men, that they may serve me.

15. Quran, Az – Zumar, 39:53

   Say: "O my servants who have transgressed against their souls! Despair not of the mercy of Allah, for Allah forgives all sins, for He is oft -forgiving, most merciful.

Note: There are 71 verses which stated these "oft -forgiving, most merciful".

16. Quran, Al – Baqarah 2:195

And spend of your substance in the cause of Allah and make not your own hands contribute (your) destruction, but do good, for Allah loveth those who do good.

17. Quran, Asy – Syuura, 42:11

(He is) the Creator of the heavens and the earth, He has made for your pairs among yourselves, and pairs among cattle, by this means does He multiply you, there is nothing whatever like unto Him, and He is the one that hears and sees (*all things).*

Note: There are 11 verses which stated these "hears and sees (all things)".

18. Quran, A-li'Imraan, 3:108

These are the signs of Allah. We rehearse them to thee in truth., and Allah means no injustice to any of His creatures.

19. Quran, An – Nisaa, 4:59

O ye who believe! Obey Allah and obey the Messenger and those charged with authority among you.

20. Quran, Al-Baqarah, 2:21

O ye people. Adore your Guardian-Lord, who created you and those who came before you, that ye may have the chance to <u>learn</u> righteousness.

Note: There are 20 verses which stated these "learn/learning".

21. Quran, A-li'Imraan, 3:92

By no means shall ye attain righteousness unless ye <u>give</u> (*freely*) of that ye love, and whatever ye give, of a truth Allah knoweth it well.

22. Quran, Al-Baqarah, 2:276

Allah will deprive usury of all blessing, but will give increase for deeds of <u>charity,</u> for He loveth not creatures ungrateful and wicked.

Note: There are 49 verses which stated these "charity".

23. Quran, Al-Muddaththir, 74:6

Nor expect in <u>giving</u>, any increase (for thyself)

24. Quran, Al – Insaan, 76: 8-9

And they feed for the love of Allah, the indigent, the orphan and the captive. (Saying) We feed you for the sake of Allah alone, <u>no reward</u> do we desire from you, nor thanks.

25. Quran, A-li'Imraan, 3:145

Nor can a soul die except by Allah leave, the term being fixed as by writing.

26. Quran, An – Nisaa', 4:124

If any do deeds of righteousness – be they male or female - and have faith, they will enter Heaven, and not the least injustice will be done to them.

27. Quran, A-li'Imraan, 3:7

He, it is Who has sent down to thee the Book. In it are verses basic or fundamental (of established meaning), they are the foundation of the Book, others are allegorical.

28. Quran, Az – Zumar, 39:18

Those who listen to the Word and follow the best (meaning) in it, those who are the ones whom Allah has guided and those are the ones endued with understanding.

29. Quran, Al – Kahfi, 18:27

And recite what has been revealed to thee of the Book of thy Lord, none can change His Words, and none wilt thou find as refuge other than Him.

30. Quran, Al – 'Alaq, 96:4

He who taught (*the use of*) the pen.

31. Quran, An-Naml, 27:3

Those who establish regular prayer and give regular charity and also have (full) assurance of the hereafter.

Note: There are 29 verses which stated these "regular prayer".

32. Quran, Al-Baqarah, 2:183

O ye who believe. Fasting is prescribed to you as it was prescribed to those before you that ye may (learn) self - restraint.

Note: There are 14 verses which stated these "fast/fasting".

33. Quran, Asy-Syuura, 42:51

It is not fitting for a man that Allah should speak to him except by inspiration or from behind a veil, or by sending of a Messenger to reveal, with Allah permission, what Allah will, for He is most high, most wise.

34. Quran, Al-Baqarah, 2:97

Say, whoever is an enemy to Gabriel – for he brings down the (*revelation*) to thy heart by Allah will, a confirmation of what went before and guidance and glad tidings for those who believe.

35. Quran, Al-Maaidah, 5:32

On that account: We ordained for the children of Israel that if anyone slew a person – unless it be for murder or for spreading mischief in the land – it would be as if he slew the whole people:

and if anyone saved a life, it would be as if he saved the life of the whole people.

36. Quran, Asy-Syuura, 42:41

But indeed, if any do help and defend themselves after a wrong (done) to them, against such there is no cause of blame.

37. Quran, Al-Baqarah, 2:190

Fight in the cause of Allah those who fight you, but do not transgress limits; for Allah loveth not transgressors.

38. Quran, An-Anfaal, 8:61

But if the enemy incline towards peace, do thou (*also*) incline towards peace, and trust in Allah, for He is One that heareth and knoweth (*all things*).

39. Quran, At-Taubah, 9:51

Say, "Nothing will happen to us except what Allah has decreed for us. He is our protector and on Allah let the believers put their trust".

40. Quran, Al-Kahfi, 18:29

Say, "The truth is from your Lord. Let him who will believe and let him who will reject (it)".

41. <u>Quran, Al-Jaathiyah, 45:13</u>

And He has subjected to you as from Him, all that in heavens and on earth. Behold, in that are signs indeed for those who reflect.

42. <u>Quran, Al-Maaidah 5:16</u>

Wherewith Allah guideth all who seek His good pleasure to ways of peace and <u>safety</u> and leadth them out of darkness, by His will, unto the light, guide them to the path that is straight.

Note: There are 16 verses which stated these "safety".

43. <u>Quran, Al-Israa' 17:82</u>

We send down (stage by stage) in the Quran that which is a <u>healing</u> and a mercy to those who believe; to the unjust it causes nothing but loss after loss.

Note: There are 9 verses which stated these "healing/heal".

44. <u>Quran, A-li'Imraan 3:186</u>

Ye shall certainly be tried and <u>tested</u> in your possessions and in your personal selves, and ye shall certainly hear much that will grieve you, from those who received the Book before you and from those who worships many gods. But if you <u>persevere patiently</u> and guard against evil, then that will be a determining factor in all affairs.

Note: There are 32 verses which stated these "test" and 14 verses which stated these "persevere patiently".

45. Quran, Al-An'aam 6:42

Before thee We sent (apostles) to many nations and We afflicted the nations with <u>suffering</u> and adversity, that they might <u>learn humility</u>.

46. Quran, Saad 38:71-72

Behold, thy Lord said to the angels: I am about to create man from clay. When I have fashioned him (*in due proportion*) and <u>breathed into him My spirit</u>, fall ye down in obeisance unto him.

Appendix B

Examples of <u>Do and Don't</u> in Quran that will lead us to be <u>safe, healthy, learning and giving</u> for the wellbeing of human being, until our destined death, for the greater good and be rewarded in Heaven for such obedience.

Do and Don't	Quran Chapter: Verse No.	Purpose (*as inferred by the author*)
Don't make excuse with God's name to not doing good or acting rightly or making peace between person and God will not call us to account but for the intention in our hearts.	2: 224-225	Giving for others' wellbeing. Our intention matters.
Don't mischief the earth	2:11, 2:27, 2:60, 2:205, 5:64, 7:56, 7:74, 7:85, 17:4, 18:94, 38:28	Ours and others' safety and health
Don't bribe	2:188	Giving (*demonstrate morality of honesty*) for others' wellbeing
Don't be arrogant	2:206, 7:146, 31:18, 40:60, 44:19, 46:20 and other 32 verses	Humility for continual learning

Do and Don't	Quran Chapter: Verse No.	Purpose (*as inferred by the author*)
Don't cheat	17:35	Giving (*demonstrate morality of honesty*) for others' wellbeing
Don't take credit for what you did not earn or deserve	3:188	Giving (*demonstrate morality of honesty*) for others' wellbeing
Don't associate partners with Allah Almighty	4:116, 17:22, 25:2, 25:68	Obedience to the one God that will guide us to the right path: be safe, healthy, learning, giving and be rewarded in heaven.
Don't be a murderer	17:33, 25:68	Others' safety
Don't take intoxicant.	5:90, 5:91	Our safety and health
Don't steal	60:12	Giving (*demonstrate morality of honesty*) for others' wellbeing
Don't utter slander	60:12, 68:11	Giving (*demonstrate morality of honesty*) for others' wellbeing
Don't be unjust	60:8 and other 42 verses.	Giving (*demonstrate morality of fairness*) for others' wellbeing.
Don't commit adultery or fornication	17:32, 24:2, 24:3, 25:68, 60:12	Our safety and health (*avoid sexual transmitted disease*) and giving (*demonstrate morality of honesty and caring of offspring in proper family*) for others' wellbeing.
No compulsion in religion	2:256	Giving (*demonstrate morality of respect others*) for others' wellbeing.

Do and Don't	Quran Chapter: Verse No.	Purpose (*as inferred by the author*)
Don't cover truth with falsehood and don't conceal the truth when ye know	2:42	Giving (*demonstrate morality of honesty*) for others' wellbeing
Don't be a bragging boaster	31:18	Humility for continual learning
Don't pursue that of which you have no knowledge.	17:36	Seek knowledge (learning)
Don't defame, don't be sarcastic to others	49:11	Giving (*demonstrate morality of respect others*) for others' wellbeing
Don't be suspicious	49:12	Seek understanding (learning)
Don't say something that you have no knowledge of it.	24: 15	Acquire knowledge (learning) and giving (*demonstrate morality of honesty*) for others' wellbeing
Lower your voice	31:19	Giving (*demonstrate morality of respect others*) for others' wellbeing
Be moderate in thy pace	31:19	Our health. Slow walk improves cardiovascular fitness, cardiovascular risk, glycemic control, stress levels and may help prevent dementia – Dr Weinrauch.
Walk with humility	25:63	Humility for continual learning
Consider others innocent until they are proven guilty	24: 11-13	Acquire knowledge (learning). Giving (*demonstrate morality of fairness*) for others' wellbeing.

Do and Don't	Quran Chapter: Verse No.	Purpose (*as inferred by the author*)
Ascertain the truth in any news	49:6	Acquire knowledge (learning)
Fulfill every engagement (*promise*), for every engagement will be enquired into.	17:34	Giving (*demonstrate morality of honesty and respect others*) for others' wellbeing
You must first practice good deeds yourself before preaching to others	2: 44	Giving (*demonstrate morality of showing good examples*) for others' wellbeing
Forgive the fault of others	24:22, 45:14	Giving (*demonstrate morality of forgiving*) for others' wellbeing
Punish those who hurt you in equal amount. Punish as you were punished, but if you show patience, it be better for you. If you forgive, then it is better	22:60, 42:40-43	Giving (*demonstrate morality of fairness, forgiving*) for others' wellbeing
It is best if you give charity to those in need in secret	2:271	Giving (*charity*) for others' wellbeing, with humility
Do good to parents, kinsfolk, orphans, those in need, neighbours, who are near, neighbours who are strangers, the companion by your side, the wayfarer and what your right hand possess.	4:36	Giving (*demonstrate morality of caring*) for others' wellbeing, starting with the ones closer to us

Printed in the United States
by Baker & Taylor Publisher Services